AGELESS ATHLETE SERIES

TENNIS
Past 50

Tony Trabert

Ron Witchey

with Don DeNevi

Human Kinetics

Library of Congress Cataloging-in-Publication Data

Trabert, Tony.
    Tennis past 50 / Tony Trabert and Ron Witchey.
        p. cm.   (Ageless Athlete Series)
    Includes bibliographical references and index.
    ISBN 0-7360-3438-2
        1. Tennis for the aged. I. Title: Tennis past fifty. II. Witchey, Ron, 1941- III. Title.
    GV1001.4.A35 T73 2001
    796.352'084'6--dc21
ISBN: 0-7360-3438-2

                                                                                        2001045796

Acquisitions Editor: Martin Barnard; **Developmental Editor:** Patricia Norris, PhD; **Managing Editor:** Wendy McLaughlin; **Assistant Editors:** Dan Brachtesende and Kim Thoren; **Copyeditor:** Christine Drews; **Proofreader:** Myla Smith; **Indexer:** Betty Frizzéll; **Permission Manager:** Toni Harte; **Graphic Designer:** Robert Reuther; **Graphic Artist:** Tara Welsch; **Cover Designer:** Keith Blomberg; **Photo Manager:** Les Woodrum; **Photographer (cover):** Tom Roberts; **Photographer (interior):** Tom Roberts, unless otherwise noted; **Art Manager:** Carl Johnson; **Illustrator:** Sharon Smith; **Printer:** United Graphics

Information on pages 12-13, 20-21, 42-43, 66-67, 84-85, 112-113, 120-121, 124-125, and 134-135 adapted courtesy of Bud Collins' *Tennis Encyclopedia.*

Printed in the United States of America   10   9   8   7   6   5   4   3   2   1

Human Kinetics
Web site: www.humankinetics.com

United States: Human Kinetics, P.O. Box 5076, Champaign, IL 61825-5076
800-747-4457
e-mail: humank@hkusa.com

Canada: Human Kinetics, 475 Devonshire Road Unit 100, Windsor, ON N8Y 2L5
800-465-7301 (in Canada only)
e-mail: orders@hkcanada.com

Europe: Human Kinetics, Units C2/C3 Wira Business Park, West Park Ring Road, Leeds
LS16 6EB, United Kingdom
+44 (0) 113 278 1708
e-mail: hk@hkeurope.com

Australia: Human Kinetics, 57A Price Avenue, Lower Mitcham, South Australia 5062
08 8277 1555
e-mail: liahka@senet.com.au

New Zealand: Human Kinetics, P.O. Box 105-231, Auckland Central
09-523-3462
e-mail: hkp@ihug.co.nz

*To all those players 50 and over who still love
the great sport of tennis.*

Contents

Preface   vii

Acknowledgments   ix

Chapter 1   **Playing Smarter, Not Harder**   **1**

Using the Warm-Up
to Scout Your Opponent 2

Knowing Your Strengths
and Weaknesses 3

The Racket Spin 4

Receiving the Serve 4

Choosing the Best Return 5

Volley Position 8

What to Do About Spin 9

The Six-Inch Difference 10

Playing on Clay 10

Mental Toughness 11

Final Thoughts 14

Chapter 2   **Upgrading Your Equipment**   **15**

Racket 16

Strings 18

Racket Grip 22

Reducing Strain and Pain 24

Shoes 25

Tennis Balls 25

Final Thoughts 26

Chapter 3   **Assessing Your Fitness
and Your Game**   **27**

Comparative Analysis of Your Strokes 28

Analyzing Your Playing Game 30

Assessing Your Fitness Level 30
About Fitness and Playing Tennis 41
Final Thoughts 44

Chapter 4   **Hitting Your Best Strokes**   **45**
Basic Grips 46
The Serve 50
Ground Strokes 52
The Volley 52
The Drop Shot 55
Returning the Drop Shot 56
The Lob 57
The Backhand 63
Footwork 68
Final Thoughts 70

Chapter 5   **Conditioning for a Stronger Game**   **71**
Conditioning Definitions 72
Strength Training 74
Muscular Endurance Training 77
Cardiovascular Endurance Training 82
Flexibility Training 86
Recovering After Play 96
Final Thoughts 97

Chapter 6   **Eating for Competition**   **99**
Setting Nutrition Goals 100
Caloric Intake Per Day 101
Six Essential Nutrients 102
Nutrition Guidelines:
    Playing a Competitive Match 110
Muscle Cramps 114
Final Thoughts 115

Chapter 7   **Winning Strategies
            for Different Opponents**   **117**
The Dinker 118
The Hard Hitter 122

The Lefty 126
The Two-Handed Backhand Hitter 126
Final Thoughts 127

Chapter 8 **Improving Your Doubles Play   129**
Picking a Good Playing Partner 131
Communication 131
Doubles Strategies 136
Final Thoughts 143

Bibliography   145
Index   149
About the Authors   153

Preface

Ah, tennis. Whether you were 5 or 50, male or female, the first time you stood on the court and hit the ball solidly, you watched it soar over the net into the atmosphere, saw it land within a mile of where you intended, and were suddenly intrigued. Then something even better happened: You sensed yourself improving slightly, getting better each time you stood on the court and swung, and you became hooked for life.

Ask any tennis player over 50! Whether you are a weekend player or a seasoned athlete, a coach, or a club pro, this book will help you better understand and play tennis in later life. We focus on components of tennis that are often overlooked after midlife, yet remain key aspects of the game. We share important insights and tips for tennis success past 50 that we have compiled over decades of coaching, playing, and researching the game we so deeply love.

In the first chapter we present tennis strategies for mature players. We show you how to play smarter, not harder. In chapter 2 we discuss modern equipment and offer suggestions for choosing the right equipment for your ability and fitness level. You can learn how to assess your fitness level, your game, and your strokes in the third chapter. In chapter 4 you will learn how to use and adapt different shots to your advantage.

In chapter 5 we explain how to develop a fitness conditioning program tailored to your needs as an older tennis player. Proper conditioning is essential for injury prevention, endurance on the court, and continued success. Because fueling the body is important for any sport, chapter 6 is devoted to nutrition. Here we discuss what to eat and drink before, during, and after play.

In chapter 7 we explain how to handle various types of opponents. The dinker, the hard hitter, the left-handed player, and the two-handed backhand hitter all require different responses on the court. We discuss playing doubles in chapter

8. As players age, doubles play becomes more attractive for both the social aspects and the sharing of exertion.

There is not a greater, more challenging sport than tennis among a nicer, more gentle, self-realizing people. And, wonderfully, the largest growing segment of the tennis-playing population is over 50. Tennis is truly a lifelong sport, and *Tennis Past 50* will guide you to lifelong tennis enjoyment and success.

Acknowledgments

We would like to acknowledge Patricia Norris for her help and guidance in getting this book into print.

Thanks also to Marilyn Prigge, who was very helpful with the testing and data collection for the fitness research.

Playing Smarter, Not Harder

*None of us can scamper after shots the way
we could when we were 25. Know what?
Neither can our opponents.*

Seasoned tennis players and newcomers—those who have enjoyed the competition for decades and those who have recently fallen in love with the game—know one thing: Every stroke, every hit (whether solid or not), every set and match (whether won or lost) is preparation for the next.

For some, however, the age of 50 signals a turning point, the magic year to begin slowing down—sliding, if you will. You might think, *Well, I've reached my peak. Now, to avoid injuries, I'll take it easy and play less. I'll stop analyzing my opponent and self-regulating my game. There's no longer any reason for me to focus on mental issues like building my confidence or keeping my head in the game.*

We believe quite the opposite! Rather than relaxing and taking the game less seriously, a person past 50 should study tennis more than ever, thinking harder and more wisely than ever before. Indeed, your entire past is the foundation for the future, and you could be playing tennis for another 50 years!

You're over 50 and you can't hit the ball as hard as you once did. To add to your concerns, moving around the court isn't as easy as it once was. Bummer? Not necessarily!

The key is to play smarter—using your head and tennis knowledge to save your legs. None of us can scamper after shots the way we could when we were 25. Know what? Neither can our opponents.

Using the Warm-Up to Scout Your Opponent

As you warm up before a match, study your opponent. Watch his or her racket preparation, stroke production, and footwork. You can learn valuable information about your opponent's tendencies and habits.

Are his ground strokes stronger than his volleys? Does she hit serves flat or with a slice? Does your opponent hit topspin on the forehand side and slice on the backhand side? By studying these things, you will know where to focus your attack.

Say your opponent hits topspin on the forehand and slice on the backhand. You may want to direct your shots at his or her backhand side because balls that are hit with a slice are likely to rise and float, which makes for easier volleys.

Knowing how your opponent plays will help improve the way you play—and it could help you win!

Knowing Your Strengths and Weaknesses

Not only should you know what your opponent's strengths and weaknesses are, but you should also be aware of your own

Using a western grip, as shown here, with the racket head low, this player will hit up and over the ball imparting topspin.

strengths and weaknesses. Try to establish a game that allows you to use your strengths as much as possible. If you have a strong forehand, position yourself on the court so that you can use your forehand as often as possible. If you are in great shape and have long-lasting concentration and patience, you may want to keep the ball in play and force your opponent to try a lower-percentage shot.

Focus on what your strengths and weaknesses are today, not what they were yesterday or what they may be in the future. Keep yourself in the present. Be realistic!

The Racket Spin

When you win the spin of the racket at the beginning of a match, you probably choose to serve. We suggest another option: Receive. There are several reasons for electing to receive.

First, if you are a little nervous at the start of a match, chances are your opponent is too. If you have your opponent serve first, you may get a free point or two as a result of those anxious efforts.

Second, having your opponent serve first gives you a chance to break a sweat and get your early jitters out. This will help when it is your turn to serve.

Best of all, it doesn't cost you anything if you lose that first game. You'll be on serve next, and you'll have had a good opportunity for an early break—plus the time to settle down and work through your early-match nerves.

Try it. This tactic may work for you.

Receiving the Serve

When it comes to the serve, most club players try to hit their first serve as hard as they can; when it misses, they dink their second serve in hopes they won't serve a double fault. Be sure to adjust your court position when receiving serve. If your adversary hits the first serve hard, stand on the baseline and see if you can return the first serve consistently. If not, take a step behind the baseline to get a little more time to react to the fast serve.

If the first serve is a fault, automatically move one step inside the baseline to receive the second serve, which probably will be softer and land short in your service court. You may even be able to advance farther into the court, taking the second serve earlier and higher on the bounce. This position will provide a better angle into your opponent's court. And if you can hit the ball deep to the backhand, being closer to the net will be more effective because your opponent will have less time to get to your shot and make a decent reply.

Choosing the Best Return

You've scouted your opponent during the warm-up. You've assessed your opponent's strengths and weaknesses, and you know your own. You've won the racket spin and elected to receive. You've returned the serve successfully and now are in the middle of a rally. By carefully selecting returns, you can win the game without sacrificing your body. Try one of these effective strategies:

- Hit deep.
- Select down-the-middle or angled shots wisely.
- Hit to the backhand.
- Use shots you don't like to return.

Hit Deep

One of the most effective strategies in tennis at any age is to hit the ball consistently deep. Your deep ball will make your opponent back up well behind the baseline, forcing the return to travel a greater distance to you, which will give you more time to respond.

Players often make a key mistake when trying to hit the ball deep. Pretend someone is standing behind you, urging, "Deeper, hit it deeper." What's the first thing that comes to your mind? You probably translate the instruction into, "Harder, hit it harder." But if you were to shoot a bullet at a target and it landed lower than you intended, would you try to shoot the next bullet "harder" or "faster"? Obviously the answer is no. Instead, you would aim higher.

In an effort to get your shots deep in your opponent's court, you don't necessarily have to hit the ball harder—just aim higher over the net. In doing so, you'll achieve ample clearance over the dreaded net, and your shots will land deeper. Getting your shots to land deep in your opponent's court is a combination of trajectory and pace. Focus on the trajectory—aiming higher—and the ball will probably go deep.

Select Down-the-Middle or Angled Shots Wisely

When you are in a rally and behind the baseline, hit the ball back down the middle of the court. This will cut down the possible angles for your opponent, which means you won't have to run as far, so that you'll get to a lot more balls.

During your rally, wait for the first short return so that you can make your return from well inside the baseline. That is when you should try to hit an outright winner. If you can hit an angled shot from your short position to the corner of your opponent's service court, it will probably be a winner. Another option is to hit deep into the corner, preferably into the backhand corner. Generally, a player's backhand is weaker than his forehand. If you know your opponent's forehand is weaker, then it makes sense to attack that side instead.

If you're more comfortable hitting crosscourt than down the line, hit the ball crosscourt, even if it's directed into the stronger wing of your opponent. You are more apt to consistently make a good shot because it's your better shot. When making an angled shot of any type, if you can't hit the winner, you can at least get your opponent in trouble so that his or her return will be weak and easy for you to put away.

Did you get all of that? Hit down the middle if you are returning a long shot from behind the baseline. If you are returning a short shot, try to hit it at an angle so that it lands in the corner of your opponent's service court. If you can't do that comfortably, drive the ball deep into the corner and set yourself up in a good volleying position. Hit the ball down the line if you can, but if your crosscourt shots are better, hit it crosscourt.

Hit to the Backhand

Another strategy for returns is to hit to the backhand. Suppose you're in a rally and are uncertain where to hit your next shot. Try hitting the ball to your opponent's backhand. If your shot goes fairly deep, you'll inevitably receive a short return or a ball floating over the net, which will allow you to rush forward and put the ball away. The floater should always be taken in the air as a volley. This allows you to continue to the net to make the winning shot.

Sounds simple, huh? Maybe not, but it sure is fun trying.

Use Shots You Don't Like to Return

In all likelihood, your opponent doesn't like the same shots you don't like. For example, most people find it difficult to return a high bouncing ball on the backhand. How about a low return at your shoe tops as you're coming to the net? Nor do many of us enjoy returning softly hit shots, because we have to swing harder to generate pace. If we swing hard, we're more apt to make an error. And who likes to have to make an overhead smash from deep in the court?

If you don't like it, your adversary probably doesn't either. Try to incorporate some of these shots into your game plan. Hit to the backhand, aim to the shoes if your opponent is approaching the net, hit the ball softly to force an error on the return, or hit a high, deep lob. If these returns give you trouble in a match, then they'll probably cause trouble for the person on the other side of the net too.

Volley Position

When you advance to the net, don't stand too close. Remember that the ideal volleying position is not quite halfway from the service line to the net. If you're closer than that, it's much too easy for your opponent to lob over your head. If you are tall, you may be able to play a little closer to the net. But remember that the closer you are to the net, the less time you have to react, so be ready! From your normal volleying position, if your opponent is still getting lobs over your head, back up a step or two so you can handle the lobs more easily.

When you take the lob away from your opponent, he or she will have to try something else and will probably not be as confident with the second choice. Remember that you should always try to take your opponents' favorite shots away from them. If you cover your opponents' favorite shots, handily returning them, they will be forced to try a secondary shot, which won't be as successful.

Now that you know your ideal volleying position, consider moving from there to make other volleys. For example, if you get a high, soft shot, move forward as quickly as you can to hit an angled volley away for a winner. By moving forward as fast as you can, you'll be able to take your volley from a closer position to the net, and the ball will be higher than if you had waited for it to come to you. You'll have a much easier volley to put away.

Once you've made your volley, don't stand around admiring it! Your opponent may surprise you by returning your shot. Quickly get back to your volleying position. The placement of your volley should help you decide where to position yourself for the next volley. If you placed your volley to one of the deep corners, quickly get back into a position that is slightly off center on the same side you hit the volley to. For example, if you placed your volley to the deep left corner of your opponent (your right), immediately position yourself slightly right of center on your side of the court. This will put you in the center of your opponent's possible returns. You should position yourself immediately in case your opponent surprises you by returning your shot. Make sure your shot bounces twice on your opponent's side before you relax!

What to Do About Spin

The average player likes a "straight ball," not a "curve ball." If you can learn to slice your serve, it will curve in flight, and on faster courts it will continue to curve after it bounces. Your opponent will probably have a difficult time figuring out how much your slice will curve. As a result, your opponent will be more likely to make an error, or misjudge or mis-hit the return, which will give you an easier shot to return. Try to use spin to your advantage, whether it is from your serve or from a ground stroke.

For a moment, let's reverse the situation. Say your opponent has an effective slice serve. If we assume that both of you are right-handed, the most effective serve is a slice wide in the first court. But what should you do if your opponent is giving you trouble with that wide delivery, by either acing you or pulling you out of the court? Take a position farther to your right than you normally would. You might straddle the singles sideline, standing on your baseline. From there you will be able to cut off the wide serve before it takes you out of position. The best way to cut off the serve is to move diagonally forward to make your return. You'll make contact before the ball can veer too wide and carry you off the court, and probably out of the point.

In addition, when you stand wider in the deuce court, it appears you're giving the server a big opening down the middle. And you are. But remember that a slice serve starting down the middle will curve toward you. If your opponent can successfully slice wide serves to you in the deuce court, and then bang a hard serve straight down the middle, you're in big trouble and undoubtedly in the wrong league!

Remember, your opponent has been hurting you with the slice serve wide in the deuce court. It's obviously his or her favorite serve. So why not take that serve away from your opponent by standing wide enough so that the slice is no longer a problem for you to handle? Now your opponent will have to go to serve B. Don't forget, it's serve B because it's not as good as serve A (the slice serve wide), so it will be easier for you to handle.

In the second court, a right-handed server will probably try to slice the serve down the middle, the equivalent to the wide serve in the deuce court. This slice serve will curve *away* from you, so be alert. Stand a little more to your right than normal. Of course, the serve down the middle in the second court will travel over the lowest part of the net, which will give the server a better chance to get it in. Remember that fact when you're serving.

The Six-Inch Difference

By the way, did you know the net is 36 inches high in the middle and 42 inches high over the sidelines? A huge six-inch difference! Shots down the middle have a better chance of going over the net than those attempted down the line. The same goes, of course, for passing shots when your opponent is at the net. Your crosscourt passing shots are more likely to clear the lower part of the net than are any attempts to pass down the line. This doesn't mean you shouldn't try a shot down the line from time to time. Just don't forget the higher part of the net. Food for thought!

Playing on Clay

Because playing on a clay court is a much slower game, you must pick your shots very carefully when attacking the net. On a clay court the ball tends to bounce more slowly and sit up a bit higher than it does on faster surfaces, such as grass and cement. The ball doesn't scoot through or past your opponent as quickly, so if you attack in error, your opponent will be able to return the shot, get it past you, and take the point.

Make sure you are in a position where the shot you hit will hurt your opponent enough to set you up for the put-away. When the ball lands short in your court, be aggressive and decisive in taking the net. If you watch top professional players who are not considered great volleyers, such as Andre Agassi, they are successful at the net on clay because when they attack they come at the right time from a good court position. This allows them to hit a devastating, forceful shot. This, in turn, puts the opponent in a difficult defensive position, creating a weak response and making the put-away simple.

Mental Toughness

We have discussed a lot of strategy in this chapter, but as you know, tennis is very much a mental game. Are you mentally tough? Do you control your mind or does your opponent control it? Do you control the game or does the game control you?

We firmly believe the saying, "The mind is never neutral. It either works for you or against you."

Learn to make your mind work for you. Compliment your opponent for a good shot instead of chastising yourself for a bad one. This will keep you up—you will forget the error you've just made, and you will be able to concentrate more effectively on the next point. Try not to dwell on a point that is history. Concentrate on the point at hand. Don't let what your opponent does bother you. And if it does, don't let your opponent know it! If your opponent figures out he's gotten to you, he will have a great advantage over you.

If you get down on yourself, your game will get worse. Instead, control your mind in a positive way, and you will only get better. This takes practice. Just like learning a forehand, it won't happen overnight.

Overcoming psychological obstacles effortlessly is, of course, a mental task and not very easy. But tennis players past 50 have some advantages. Their matches are usually friendly. They play with little pressure and for the sheer fun of it. Even losing has few ill consequences.

Yet, the goal should be to win. To do that, you must resolve to implement these mental strategies:

- Consider each and every point an "exchange," a "dance," really, with your opponent—one in which you enjoy each other's movements and yet work to win the point.

BILLIE JEAN KING

Citizenship: United States of America

Best known for: Winning 20 Wimbledon Championships

© AP Photo

Billie Jean King was a tremendous athlete who moved extremely well. She had an all-court game and constantly sought opportunities to attack. An outstanding volleyer, she was aggressive and, at times, very emotional on the court. She was a very good tactician and had the ability to adjust her game and, as a result, was able to win on any surface.

Billie Jean will always be remembered for her victory over Bobby Riggs in the "Battle of the Sexes" in 1973. In my opinion, no one has done more for women's rights than Billie Jean King—for women's sports in general, but especially in tennis. Her talent, enthusiasm, and vigor, more than anyone at the time, popularized women's professional tennis.

Billie Jean King was inducted into the International Tennis Hall of Fame in 1987.

Accomplishments

39 Grand Slam titles (12 singles; 16 doubles; 11 mixed doubles)
Australian (1 single; 1 mixed)
French (1 singles; 1 double; 2 mixed)
Wimbledon (6 singles; 10 doubles; 4 mixed)
US Open (4 singles; 5 doubles; 4 mixed)

—Tony Trabert

- Relax on the court and realize that the competition is really between you and yourself. In a sense you have a new start after each point because you are focusing on playing the point, not your opponent.

- Practice a personal resoluteness in being proactive rather than reactive, patiently watching and waiting for the first short ball so that you can attack it, developing that certain mental coldness to think calmly and rationally while on the court.

- Never fret about the past point regardless of how irritating your error or how bad a call. Let it be said that you didn't think about what would come next, that you focused with icy calm on the moment and the ball. Let it be said how tough you are.

- Honestly believe that if you play well, the breaks will go your way.

Final Thoughts

This chapter has been filled with fun ideas to think about. We hope you've learned a few new tricks along the way—from making a different choice at the racket spin to choosing the best return. Maybe you have learned something new about positioning yourself to receive the serve or advancing to the net to volley. And yet with all these strategies in mind, we know tennis is as much a mental game as it is a physical competition. As we've said, "Play smarter, not harder." But in the end, don't forget to have fun in the process!

chapter

2

Upgrading Your Equipment

Most players over 50 have less power than they had when they were 25. If this sounds like you, choose a racket that is stiffer and wider. You'll get more power with less effort.

Many older players can improve their games by taking inventory of their equipment and assessing how well it is working. Tennis equipment manufacturers have made great technological advances. It may be time to retire that sentimental old racket and buy a new pair of shoes.

Racket

In today's world of high-tech material and equipment, you can find a racket tailor-made for you. You have many options to choose from. Graphite? Braided graphite? Hyper carbon? Titanium? It can be overwhelming. Don't make the decision by yourself. Seek the guidance and expertise of your local tennis professional.

Swing Speed

As you look for the perfect racket for you, consider your swing speed. For example, if you have a short, compact swing along with a slow swing speed, choose a racket that is stiffer and wider. A stiffer, wider racket will give you more power with less effort. This will give you the additional power you need to offset your slower swing speed.

On the other hand, if you have a long, loopy, full swing with a fast swing speed, choose a racket that is thinner and more flexible. Thinner, more flexible rackets give you more control and less power. Because of the flexibility in the frame, the racket actually deadens the speed of the ball at impact. This will allow you to swing aggressively and yet control the ball so that it stays in the same zip code. This type of racket is often referred to as a "player's" racket.

Racket manufacturers produce a wide range of rackets to cover the wide range of swing speeds. Most players over 50 have less power than they had when they were 25. If this sounds like you, choose a racket that is stiffer and wider. You'll get more power with less effort.

Racket Length

Today's rackets come in sizes longer than the old standard of 27 inches, to 27.5, 28, and even 28.5 inches. In fact, the maximum length of a tennis racket permitted by today's rules is 29 inches. That may not sound like much, but that small bit of length can make a big difference in your serve and in your ground strokes.

Typically a longer racket adds power at the expense of control. The extra reach can give you more options on the serve—it's as if you suddenly became taller. And if you need some extra zip on your shots, a longer racket might be just what you've been looking for. What if you find you need more control on your ground strokes but still want the longer racket for your serves? Try adding more tension to the strings so that you can reap the benefits of the extra reach on the serve yet have control on your ground strokes. You might also try choking up on the handle when hitting shots other than your serve.

Be sure to try several different brands and models in long rackets because their power and control can vary significantly.

Racket Head Size

As you evaluate your racket or look for a new one, also consider the size of the racket head. The face of the racket cannot be more than 12.5 inches in overall width, and the hitting surface cannot be more than 15.5 inches long and 11.5 inches wide. The larger hitting area has enabled the current players to produce much more topspin on their ground strokes than was possible with the standard wooden racket. The new rackets offer more hitting surface with which to brush up the back of the ball to impart excessive spin.

The stiffness, balance, and weight of the racket head all affect the size of the sweet spot. If you play with a smaller head (85 to 95 square inches), you have to be much more precise. A smaller head is much less forgiving on off-center hits. The larger the racket head is, the more room you have for error. Today's big-headed rackets can give you considerable power even on off-center hits. You can actually hit relatively solid, successful shots from areas other than the middle of your strings.

Racket Weight

Racket weight has changed significantly over the years. At one time, author Tony Trabert played with a racket that had a five-inch handle, and, though evenly balanced, weighed 15 to 15.5 ounces. With the advent of stronger materials, rackets were made lighter, with larger heads and perimeter weighting. It got to the point where some people were playing with rackets as light as 8 ounces, and those rackets needed mass in the head in order to generate any power.

Now the pendulum has swung back to rackets for recreational players weighing 9 and 10 ounces. Junior and college players usually play with rackets that weigh between 11 and 12 ounces. Players on the pro circuit normally use rackets that weigh between 12 and 13 ounces with a midsized head.

People have long been concerned that playing with a very light racket might contribute to arm problems because of the vibration at impact. Because of this, many manufacturers incorporated vibration-dampening components in the design of their rackets.

As a player over 50, you should consider the consequences of playing with a racket of a particular weight. If you have arm or elbow injuries, you might want to use a slightly heavier racket or one with vibration-dampening features. If you compete regularly, you might also opt for a heavier racket—perhaps one that weighs 11 or 12 ounces. But most recreational players over 50 prefer rackets in the 9- to 10-ounce range.

Strings

Remember the days when your choice of strings was either gut or nylon? Well, those days are long gone. Oh, both of those types of strings are still around, but now we also have an array of synthetic materials to choose from. There is still nothing quite like natural gut string, but some of the new strings come close. You can choose among strings that are softer and absorb shock better; strings that are more durable, more playable, and give you more spin; or strings that combine the best of both worlds. You can find a string that will give you just what you're looking for.

There is no set answer for how often you should restring your racket, but the industry rule of thumb is to restring your racket each year the same number of times you play per week. For example, if you play twice a week, you should get your racket restrung twice a year.

Often, the strings look fine but still need to be replaced. Over time, they lose their resilience and feel dead, even when they look like new. If you haven't had your racket restrung for a while, it's probably time to do so. You will be amazed at what a fresh set of strings will do for your game.

String Tension

How tightly should you string your racket? That's a very good question: Tension is the most important aspect of dealing with string.

The actual tension with which you string your racket is up to you, but you should base the tension on your swing speed. Contrary to popular belief, you do not get more power from a tightly strung racket and more control from a loosely strung racket. It's just the opposite. You get more power and less control when a racket is strung at lower tensions, and less power with more control when it is strung at higher tensions.

Visualize a trampoline versus a brick wall. When the ball hits the strings of a loosely strung racket, the strings act like a trampoline. The strings give and then catapult the ball off the racket, giving your shot more speed and power but less control. When the ball hits the strings of a tightly strung racket, the strings act like a brick wall. The strings don't give; instead, the ball gives and compresses, which deadens the power. At the same time, though, the strings flatten, which gives you more feel and control.

Citizenship: Australia

Best known for: Winning 13 Grand Slam titles

© Sarah J. Vickery/HENMAGIC

Evonne Goolagong was among the most graceful movers and players that tennis has ever known. She ran like a gazelle and the ball seemed to flow off her racket. It was if she played the game by instinct.

She liked to serve and volley, which, combined with her speed and agility, gave her the ability to cover the net beautifully. At times her attention would waiver and she would go "walk-about," allowing unforced errors to occur. However, her happy, free-willed spirit and pleasant attitude on the court always made her a pleasure to watch.

Evonne Goolagong Cawley was inducted into the International Tennis Hall of Fame in 1988.

Accomplishments

13 Grand Slam titles (7 singles; 5 doubles; 1 mixed doubles)
Australian (4 singles; 4 doubles)
French (1 single; 1 mixed)
Wimbledon (2 singles; 1 doubles)

—Tony Trabert

So, if you swing easily and slowly, you should string your racket more loosely. The loose tension will give you more power with less effort. But if you swing fast and aggressively, you should string your racket a little tighter. This will help deaden the ball at impact, giving you less power but more control over your shot.

Finally, if you have an arm problem, such as tennis elbow or a sore wrist or shoulder, use a looser tension. The loose strings will help absorb the shock of the ball at impact, sparing your arm.

String Gauge

Strings come in different widths or gauges, anywhere from 15 gauge to 19 gauge. The lower the number, the thicker, more durable, and less lively the string. The higher the number, the thinner, less durable, more lively the string. Think about what you're looking for in your game and from your string before you buy. For example, if you've had tennis elbow, you want to look for a string that will absorb a lot of shock and be soft on your arm—maybe an 18- or 19-gauge string.

Racket Grip

In my opinion, 95 percent of the people playing tennis have too small a grip on their rackets. Use these two methods to assess your grip size:

1. Grip your racket and see if you can fit one finger between the ends of your fingers and the meaty part below your thumb. If you can't, the grip on your racket is probably too small.

2. Grip your racket and see if the end of your thumb goes past the first knuckle of your middle finger. If it does, your racket grip is too small for your hand.

If your racket grip is too small, the racket is apt to turn in your hand on a miss hit, and you won't have the feel you would enjoy with a larger grip size.

Incorrect grip size—the grip is too small. The thumb goes past the first knuckle of the middle finger.

Correct grip size—thumb should come to the first knuckle of the middle finger.

If you discover that your grip is too small, don't go out and buy a new racket. A club pro can build the grip by removing your leather grip and putting strips of tape on each bevel. Don't let anyone just wrap tape around your grip because that will make the handle feel too round.

Talk to your club pro or the staff at a sporting goods store about the racket you are using. Is it too stiff? Is it too light? Is it strung at a tension that suits your game? The professional's answers and suggestions will help you upgrade your equipment.

Reducing Strain and Pain

A combination of proper technique and high-tech equipment can help you reduce strain and pain. Be sure to use proper grips when you play. For example, many players use a forehand grip to hit their backhand. This causes great shock and strain to tendons in your elbow. If you change your dominant hand to the proper grip (Eastern backhand), it'll give you more support to counteract the impact of the ball and reduce the strain on your elbow.

You can also reduce strain to your elbow by making contact with the ball in front of your body on all shots, while maintaining a firm grip. Try to avoid hitting the ball late or behind your body.

Today's technology provides many products to help our joints. Vibration dampeners and rackets with vibration-dampening components in the grip or racket head are great. In addition, many of today's strings are designed to be soft on the arm. If you experience elbow problems, ask one of the pros or an expert at the sporting goods store for a soft string, and string your racket on the loose side (55 pounds or lower).

Using a combination of proper technique and appropriate equipment should help reduce existing pain and prevent tennis elbow altogether.

Shoes

As with other tennis equipment, shoes have come a long way, with new designs that are highly technical and performance oriented. Soles are now made of different types of rubber compounds for increased durability. Manufacturers put air in the forefoot, air in the heel, and air in both the forefoot and heel. You can find low-tops, mid-tops, polyurethane midsoles, designs that wrap around your foot for added stability, and even speed lacing. You can buy shoes specifically made for hard courts, clay courts, and grass courts. Upgrading to a new high-performance shoe is well worth the investment. Many shoe manufacturers continue to offer wear guarantees and will replace shoes that wear out prematurely.

Tennis shoes for women are different from those of men. In the past, some manufacturers simply made men's shoes smaller in order to sell them to women. Today, manufacturers sell shoes specifically designed for women. Women's shoes are typically wider in the forefoot and more narrow in the heel, whereas men's shoes are similar in width in the forefoot and heel. As we get older, our feet usually grow bigger and wider. So try on different tennis shoe brands to determine what suits your feet best. Shoes on the market today are made so well, choosing the best one is like choosing between a red Ferrari and a blue Ferrari.

Tennis Balls

Not all tennis balls are the same. Although all tennis balls must fit within certain parameters of size, weight, and pressure, balls are made for different specific purposes. Balls made for hard courts have longer felt to prolong the wear. Balls made for grass courts have shorter felt. Felt collects grass stain, and grass stain adds weight, so that balls with shorter felt collect less stain than do balls with more nap, making them suitable for grass courts.

For high altitudes, a pressureless ball can be used. The lack of pressure helps to counteract the thinner air. The thin air allows a pressurized tennis ball to travel faster than it would at a lower altitude. If you played at a high altitude with a regular tennis ball, you would feel as if you were playing with a golf ball. It would be very difficult to control serving, volleying, or hitting ground strokes.

Final Thoughts

The game is tough enough. So give yourself every opportunity possible to be successful. Be sure to get professional help regarding which racket you should use, of which weight and balance, correct head size, and what kind of string and what tension. These are all very important factors in helping you to be the best player you can be.

chapter

3

Assessing Your Fitness and Your Game

Have you ever wondered how your strokes compare to those of the top players? In a match, do you know what percentage of winners you hit with your ground strokes, serves, volleys, and returns of serves? How does your fitness level compare to that of other senior tennis players and even older adults who do not play tennis? In this chapter, we will show you how to assess these aspects of your fitness and your game.

Comparative Analysis of Your Strokes

One way to analyze your strokes is to compare video of your playing to video or sequential photos of the top players. Videos and sequential photos of most of the top players are available online, in book stores, in magazines such as *Tennis*, or in books.

First look at the video or photos of the pros. Break the stroke down into phases: stance, backswing, forward swing, contact point, and follow-through. Break the body down into five segments: feet, legs, hips and shoulders, arms and hands, and head. As you look at each phase of the stroke, ask the following questions about each body segment. You will likely see some similar patterns in each phase of the stroke, even in a variety of pro players.

Now have someone videotape you while you're hitting. Ask the person to videotape you from a side view and either a front or back view. This will help you see each body part clearly.

Questions to Ask

Ask the same questions about each phase of the stroke as you asked about the pros' strokes, and compare yourself to the pro models for each stroke.

Feet

1. What is the position of the feet (staggered, parallel, together)?

2. Where is the body weight distributed on the feet (front, right, left, back, inside, outside)?

3. What is the movement or pattern of the feet (split step, crossover, open or closed stance)?

4. What is the position of the ball at contact (off front foot, in front of front foot)?

Legs

1. What is the position of the legs (close together, wide apart)?

2. How flexed are the knees and hip joints?

Hips and Shoulders

1. What is the position of the hips in relation to the shoulders?

2. What is the position of the hips and shoulders in relation to the surrounding area (facing the net, facing the sideline)?

3. What is the sequence of movement of the hips with the shoulders (do shoulders turn first, then hips)?

4. When do the shoulders turn (as ball goes over net, as player is setting up)?

Arms and Hands

1. What type of grip is used?

2. What is the position of the racket arm and nonracket arm?

3. Is there a loop in the backswing? If so, what type of loop is it (big, small, fast, slow)?

4. What is the movement pattern of each arm? When do the arms separate or move together?

Head

1. What is the position of the head (looking up or down, behind the ball)?

2. Where are the eyes focused?

By systematically comparing your movements to those of pro players, you'll be able to see which parts of your strokes you can work on.

Analyzing Your Playing Game

You can analyze the strengths and weaknesses of your playing game by developing an analysis chart on which to track your stroke errors and winners. Once you have developed a chart, have someone watch you play a match and record your stroke errors and winners. You can set up the chart to record whatever aspects of the game you want to analyze. You can see an example of such a chart on page 31.

After your match has been charted, you can calculate your percentage of winners and errors, just as they do in the pros. You can determine the percentage of first serves in on both the deuce and ad courts. You can also determine the percentage of points won on forehands, backhands, volleys, overheads, returns of serve, and so forth. Keeping track of how you play a match will help you see parts of the game that you need to improve. You will get a clear picture of your strengths and weaknesses. This feedback can help you develop a program to improve your game, whether you coach yourself or seek advice from a teaching pro.

Assessing Your Fitness Level

Have you ever wondered if playing tennis is keeping you fit? Does playing tennis give you enough and the right kind of exercise to help you lead an active and productive life? Recent research has demonstrated that tennis is effective in helping people perform everyday activities safely and effectively. If you are interested in comparing your fitness level with that of other older adults, try the following battery of fitness tests developed at the Ruby Gerontology Center at California State University at Fullerton.

TENNIS MATCH ANALYSIS CHART

Opponent _____ Score _____ Weather _____

Type of court/condition _____

Errors	Forehand	Backhand	FH volley	BH volley	Overhead	FH, midcourt	BH, midcourt
Long out							
Net ball							
Wide out							
Short ball							
Points won							

Serves	Deuce court in	Deuce court out	Ad court in	Ad court out	Percentage in		
1st serves							
2nd serves							

Returns	Deuce court in	Deuce court out	Ad court in	Ad court out	Percentage in		
1st serves							
2nd serves							

Personal comments about match:

Take the following tests, record your results, and compare them to the graphs provided with each test. The graphs show normative scores of three age groups at three different levels of activity; (1) tennis players who played tennis at least twice a week; (2) "high active" subjects, who exercised three or more times a week—exercise that typically involved walking or calisthenics at a local senior center; and (3) "low active" subjects, who got little or no exercise. Have fun with the testing and comparing!

Lower-Body Strength and Endurance

1. Chair stand and sit

Use the chair stand test to measure your lower-body strength and endurance. Sit in a chair with your lower back touching the back of the chair. Cross your arms over your chest. Count

Chair stand and sit.

the number of times within 30 seconds that you can rise to a full stand from this seated position, without pushing off with your arms. You must keep your arms crossed on your chest, and you must let your lower back touch the back of chair every time you sit down. The graph provides the normative scores for the chair stand test and a place to record your own score.

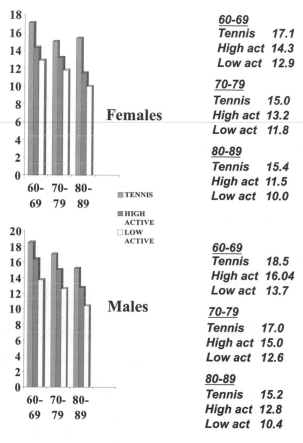

60-69
Tennis 17.1
High act 14.3
Low act 12.9

70-79
Tennis 15.0
High act 13.2
Low act 11.8

80-89
Tennis 15.4
High act 11.5
Low act 10.0

60-69
Tennis 18.5
High act 16.04
Low act 13.7

70-79
Tennis 17.0
High act 15.0
Low act 12.6

80-89
Tennis 15.2
High act 12.8
Low act 10.4

Normative scores for the chair stand and sit.

Upper-Body Strength and Endurance

2. Arm curl

To measure your upper-body strength and endurance, take the arm curl test. If you are a female, use a 5-pound dumbbell. If you are a male, use an 8-pound dumbbell. Using your racket arm, curl the dumbbell through a full range of motion as many times as you can in 30 seconds. Keep your torso erect and your upper arm stationary. Record your 30-second total on the graph. Compare your score to the norms. How did you do?

Arm curl.

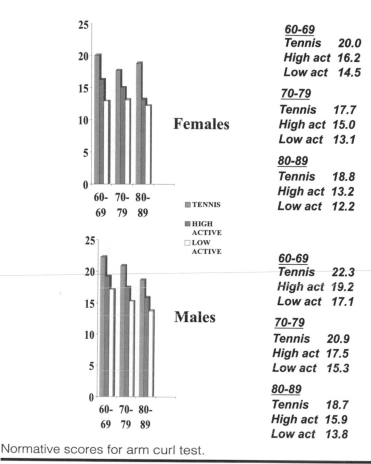

60-69
Tennis   20.0
High act 16.2
Low act   14.5

70-79
Tennis   17.7
High act 15.0
Low act   13.1

80-89
Tennis   18.8
High act 13.2
Low act   12.2

60-69
Tennis   22.3
High act 19.2
Low act   17.1

70-79
Tennis   20.9
High act 17.5
Low act   15.3

80-89
Tennis   18.7
High act 15.9
Low act   13.8

Normative scores for arm curl test.

Aerobic Endurance

3. Two-minute step test

To determine aerobic endurance, take the two-minute step test. Unlike some step tests, this one does not involve stepping up onto a bench or step. Instead, this test involves determining the number of times, within two minutes, that you can step in place, raising the knees to a height half the distance between your hipbone and the top of your kneecap. Each time the right knee comes up to the proper height, count it as one step. (A left-right cadence equals one step count.) Make sure you pace yourself. Two minutes is longer than you think! You may not run in place; you must walk. If needed, you can rest and resume your count until the two minutes are up. Check out the graph to see how you compare to other older adults.

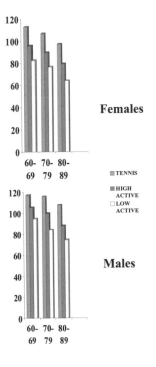

Two-minute step test.

Females

60-69
Tennis   112.8
High act   95.9
Low act   8.24

70-79
Tennis   106.7
High act   89.7
Low act   76.7

80-89
Tennis   97.4
High act   79.7
Low act   76.7

TENNIS
HIGH ACTIVE
LOW ACTIVE

Males

60-69
Tennis   117.0
High act   105.4
Low act   94.7

70-79
Tennis   115.6
High act   99.8
Low act   84.2

80-89
Tennis   107.7
High act   87.9
Low act   74.6

Normative scores for two-minute step test.

Agility and Balance

4. 8 foot up and go

To assess agility and balance, perform the 8 foot up-and-go test. Set a cone eight feet from a chair. Sit in the chair. Get out of the chair, walk (don't run) eight feet to and around the cone, and return to the chair in the shortest time possible. Remember, you cannot run. Instead, walk as fast as you can and record your best time. Record the better of two trials to the nearest tenth of a second. Compare your time with the times in the graph.

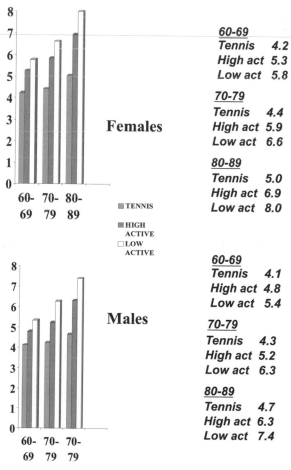

Females

■ TENNIS
■ HIGH ACTIVE
□ LOW ACTIVE

60-69
Tennis   4.2
High act   5.3
Low act   5.8

70-79
Tennis   4.4
High act   5.9
Low act   6.6

80-89
Tennis   5.0
High act   6.9
Low act   8.0

Males

60-69
Tennis   4.1
High act   4.8
Low act   5.4

70-79
Tennis   4.3
High act   5.2
Low act   6.3

80-89
Tennis   4.7
High act   6.3
Low act   7.4

Normative scores for 8 foot up-and-go test.

Lower-Body Flexibility

5. Chair sit and reach

To assess lower-body flexibility, use the chair sit-and-reach test. You'll need a friend and a ruler to help you with this test. Sit at the front edge of a chair and extend one leg straight out in front of the hip, with the foot flexed and the heel resting on the floor. The other leg should be bent, with the foot flat on the floor. With your arms, reach as far as possible toward (or past) the toes of the straight leg. Try once with one leg forward and again with the other leg forward. Select the leg forward position that feels best for you. Do two trials with the preferred leg forward. Exhale as you reach down toward your toes. Ask your friend to record with a ruler the number of inches your fingertips are short of reaching the toes (minus score) or the number of inches your fingertips reach beyond the toes (plus score). If you touch your toes, but don't reach beyond, record a score of "0." Record the better score of the two trials to the nearest half inch. How does your score compare to other scores in the graph?

Chair sit and reach.

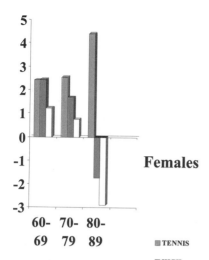

Females

TENNIS
HIGH ACTIVE
LOW ACTIVE

60-69
Tennis   2.4 in.
High act 2.4 in.
Low act   1.2in

70-79
Tennis   2.5 in.
High act 1.7 in.
Low act   0.7 in.

80-89
Tennis   4.4 in.
High act -1.7 in.
Low act   -2.9 in.

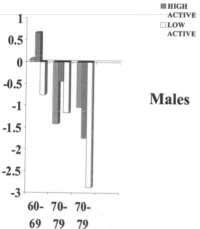

Males

60-69
Tennis   0.1 in.
High act 0.7 in.
Low act   -0.8 in.

70-79
Tennis   -1.4 in.
High act -0.4 in.
Low act   -1.2 in.

80-89
Tennis   -1.0 in.
High act -1.7 in.
Low act   -2.9 in.

Normative scores for chair sit and reach.

Upper-Body Flexibility

6. Scratch test

To evaluate upper-body flexibility, perform the scratch test. The scratch test involves measuring the distance between, or the overlap of, the middle fingers when the hands are reaching behind the back. You'll need a friend and a ruler to help you with this test. Reach behind the head with one hand and behind the back with the other hand, and try to touch the two middle fingers together behind the back. If you are right-handed, try putting your right hand behind your head and reach up with your left hand. You may want to try the reverse, but use the hand position that gives the better result. Perform two trials with your preferred hand position and record the better of the two trials. Ask your friend to measure the distance between the tips of the middle fingers or the overlap to the nearest half inch. Use a minus score if your middle fingers are short of touching; use a plus score if your middle fingers overlap. Record a score of "0" if the middle fingers of each hand touch but don't overlap. How does your flexibility score compare to the scores shown in the graph?

Scratch test.

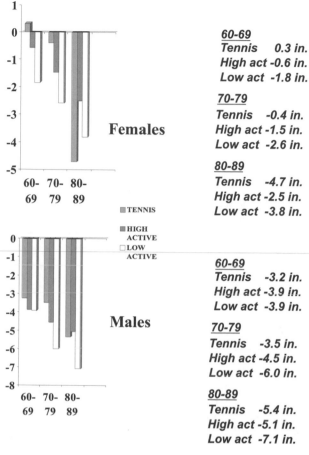

Females

60-69
Tennis   0.3 in.
High act -0.6 in.
Low act -1.8 in.

70-79
Tennis   -0.4 in.
High act -1.5 in.
Low act -2.6 in.

80-89
Tennis   -4.7 in.
High act -2.5 in.
Low act -3.8 in.

▩ TENNIS
▩ HIGH ACTIVE
☐ LOW ACTIVE

Males

60-69
Tennis   -3.2 in.
High act -3.9 in.
Low act -3.9 in.

70-79
Tennis   -3.5 in.
High act -4.5 in.
Low act -6.0 in.

80-89
Tennis   -5.4 in.
High act -5.1 in.
Low act -7.1 in.

Normative scores for scratch test.

About Fitness and Playing Tennis

For combined age groups from 60 to 89, female tennis players scored better on all six fitness tests than did "low active" or "high active" subjects. Male tennis players also scored better than both the "low active" and "high active" subjects on four of the fitness tests (lower- and upper-body strength and endurance, aerobic endurance, and agility and balance), but not on the two flexibility tests. Why are tennis players less flexible

SARAH VIRGINIA WADE

Citizenship: Great Britain

Best known for: Playing 18 years in the Federation Cup—longest on record

© Sporting Photo

Sarah Virginia Wade always had wonderful timing. She served aggressively and followed into the net where she volleyed very well. Her instincts at the net were quick and natural so she was difficult to pass. Her ground strokes were solid and her backhand more reliable than her continental forehand.

Virginia moved beautifully on the court because she was nimble and light on her feet. Ginny was agile! In 1977, she played and won in her 17th Wimbledon in front of Queen Elizabeth. There has always been a certain elegance about this wonderful champion from Great Britain.

Virginia Wade was inducted into the International Tennis Hall of Fame in 1989.

Accomplishments

7 Grand Slam titles (3 singles; 4 doubles)
Australian (1 single; 1 double)
French (1 double)
Wimbledon (1 single)
US Open (1 single; 2 doubles)

—Tony Trabert

than other older adults? Tennis players might not pay as much attention to this aspect of fitness, or they may experience increased injuries from the stress placed on the joints, muscles, and connective tissue while playing tennis. Tennis players who play tennis two or more times a week perform a majority of functional, or everyday living, tasks better than the average "low active" and "high active" senior. Playing tennis regularly appears to be a valuable physical activity for promoting fitness in later years.

What does this mean for you? If you are playing tennis two to three times a week, keep it up! If you play tennis only occasionally, you might want to increase your play to two or more times a week. Playing tennis may help you maintain a good level of fitness as you grow older.

Final Thoughts

In this chapter you have learned how to assess your strokes, match play, and fitness level. With careful analysis, you can discover which aspects of your game need improving. Often, a key to improved play is better conditioning. Read on to find out how you may be able to improve your strokes, percentages, and fitness levels with a solid conditioning program.

Hitting Your Best Strokes

If you execute a good drop shot, and your opponent
manages to barely get it back, use the offensive lob.
Chances are your opponent won't be able to recover
and get to your lob. The other person will do the
running, and you'll win the point!

Mastering and modifying several basic shots can keep you playing tennis for years. We will begin by demonstrating the basic grips and racket position, and then move on to the serve, ground strokes, the drop shot, the lob, and the smash. We'll then spend a good deal of time on the backhand and finish with a little footwork.

Basic Grips

You can choose from four fundamental grips when hitting a forehand. Often used in the forehand ground stroke is the Eastern forehand grip. The Western and Continental grips, illustrated here, are also used, as is the semi-Western grip. The final figure shows the proper hand position for the two-handed backhand grip.

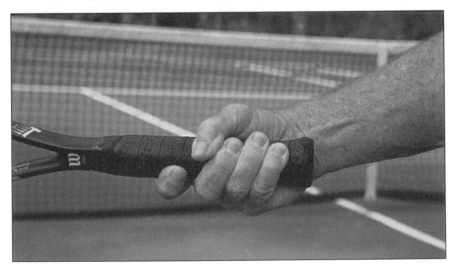

Eastern forehand grip.

Western grip.

Continental grip.

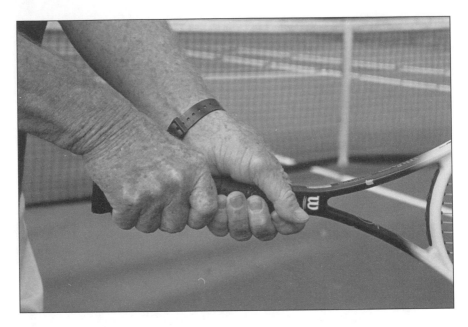

Two-handed backhand grip.

The Eastern forehand grip is also called the "shake-hands" grip. To position your hand correctly for this grip, place the palm of your hand flat on the strings of your racket and slide your hand down the shaft to the handle.

With the Eastern grip, your palm is in the same position as the racket face. Imagine hitting a ball against a wall with the palm of your hand. Swing the racket the same way, coming from slightly below the contact point and finishing high. When you start low and finish high, you hit the ball on an upward glance, and that creates topspin. This will give you a solid forehand.

The Eastern grip allows you to take the racket straight back if you are rushed, and it allows you to keep the racket behind the hitting areas. In addition, you can quickly transition from the Eastern forehand grip to a one-handed backhand: Compared with other grips, your hand has the shortest distance to rotate over the handle to get to a backhand position.

To use the semi-Western grip, slide your hand under the grip a little farther than the Eastern forehand position. This will close the face down a little, meaning it will be tilted down toward the ground. You will have to take a circular backswing with this grip because you'll have to swing from farther below the contact point and brush up the back of the ball. However, you can generate more topspin with this grip than you can with the Eastern forehand.

In the Western grip, your hand is positioned even farther under the grip, so that the racket is facing almost straight down when you're in the ready position. You'll need to use a circular backswing with this grip as well, and you'll brush up the back of the ball, starting from well below the contact point, whipping the racket head up and over the ball.

Because you are forced to take a circular backswing with the Western grip, you'll need longer to prepare for your shots. This can be a problem if a ball is hit hard at you. Also, the transition from a Western grip to a good backhand grip requires a bigger grip change than is needed from either the Eastern or semi-Western grips.

For the continental grip, roll your hand over the top of the handle, about halfway between an Eastern, or shake-hands, grip and the one-handed backhand grip.

It is very difficult to hit the forehand down the line when using the continental grip. As you contact the ball, your racket head will be slightly ahead of your hand, pointing crosscourt. To hit down the line, you'll have to let the ball get farther back, but then you won't be able to see it as well to make an effective shot.

For the most effective two-handed backhand grip, place your dominant hand (right hand, if you are right-handed) in a regular one-handed backhand grip position, and place your other hand above the lower, dominant, hand.

The upper hand helps prevent the racket head from wobbling, giving you a solid feel when you contact the ball. And with the two-hander, you can change the direction at the last second from a down-the-line shot to a crosscourt delivery by snapping your upper hand to bring the racket head through earlier.

However, with a two-handed grip, you can't reach as far as you can reach with the one-handed grip, so you'll have to run farther and faster to cover the court. You may also find it difficult to handle a short, angled ball to your backhand side when using a two-handed grip: You may be forced to let go with one hand, making the shot less effective.

The Serve

We'll look at two aspects of the serve: the toss and the swing. A good ball toss and an effective swing make for a solid serve.

The Toss

Good ball placement on the toss is the most important part of serving. Strive for consistency: If you can place the ball in the same spot each time you serve, you will be able to swing the same way each time. This makes for a better and more effective serve. If every toss is different, every swing will have to be different.

Hold the ball lightly between the first two fingers and the thumb. The fingers and thumb should be about halfway around the ball, so that you have control of it but you're not squeezing it to death. Hold your palm up (toward the sky), keep your wrist locked, and don't flick your fingers.

There is no advantage to tossing the ball higher than you can reach when you are fully stretched up, leaning slightly into the court. The ball should leave your hand around shoulder-to-head height, which means the toss should travel only three feet or so up in the air.

By the rules, the tennis ball weighs slightly less than two ounces. It doesn't take much of an arm motion to place a two-ounce ball three feet in the air. Move the tossing arm slowly and smoothly.

If you are right-handed, place your toss inside the baseline, two or three feet toward the net, and slightly to the right of your body. You'll be able to see the ball at all times as you transfer your weight into the serve. With the toss slightly to the right, you'll be able to uncoil your shoulders (like throwing a baseball) and have your racket contact the ball without your body being in the way.

If you toss the ball more to your left on a first serve, your body will restrict your serve, and you'll fall to your left on the follow-through. This is not what you want.

The only time you should toss the ball well to your left is if you are going to hit a kick serve, also called an American Twist. When kicking a serve, you arch your back and bring the racket face up and across the back of the ball, creating some topspin and sidespin. This will make the ball bounce up and away on a right-hander's backhand. Be careful trying this: The kick serve can be hard on the back!

The Swing

Swing up toward the clouds on your serve. None of us are tall enough to swing down at the ball when we serve and have it go into the service box. To do that, you would have to stand on a ladder or start a lot closer to the net. Because you can't swing down, you must learn to swing up.

If most of your serves are going into the net, you're probably hitting the top of the ball—at approximately 12 o'clock—or bending too quickly at the waist in an effort to hit the ball down into the court. Instead, you want to feel as if you are hitting the ball as your racket is on the way up and close to full extension. To fully understand this sensation, pretend you are standing at the baseline ready to serve, and you are trying to throw your racket overhand over the back fence at the opposite end of the court. You would have to throw the racket at an angle up toward the sky to have it go over the fence. This is the feeling you want on your serve.

In golf the experts say, "You have to hit down to get the ball up in the air." In tennis you must "hit up" to get the ball to clear the net with some margin of error. To get this feeling of hitting up on the ball, *sit* behind the baseline and serve the ball into the service court. When you are sitting down, the net looks high, and you may be more convinced that you should hit up on the ball to get it over the net. You will be surprised how easy it is to get the ball over the net and into the service court from a seated position. Try it!

If you can develop this type of feeling on your swing, with a good ball toss and an aggressive wrist snap, you will be hitting up on the ball, clearing the net safely, and making many more serves. Who knows? You may even get an ace or two as well.

Ground Strokes

Think about ground strokes in terms of an airplane versus a helicopter. When you watch an airplane take off what does it do? It travels down the runway, gathering speed until it begins a gradually angled ascent. A helicopter takes off vertically, or straight up.

When you are hitting forehands and backhands, pretend that your racket is an airplane, not a helicopter. As you begin your swing, the racket should travel down the runway, picking up speed as it goes. Gradually let the racket take off at an angle up in front of your body.

Avoid going partway and having your racket take off like a helicopter, going straight up in the air at a sharp angle. If you swing correctly, you'll finish with your racket hand about shoulder height out in front of your body, with your arm almost totally straight.

Using this technique gives you good extension through the hitting zone, good penetration on your shots, and topspin too.

The stroke is a gradual ascent from low to high, which gives you topspin if you keep the racket face flat or slightly closed at impact. Try it! This technique will make your ground strokes very sound.

The Volley

See chapter 1 for all the juicy details on achieving good volleying position. We'll review a little of that here and discuss the keys to an effective volleying game.

A good approach shot is the key to better volleying. If you come to the net after hitting a short, weak shot, you're just asking for trouble. But if your approach shot is forceful and deep, you will be setting yourself up for a much easier volley.

Don't decelerate on your approach shot. Always accelerate through the shot. This will help give you pace on the ball and will make your approach shot more effective. If you are well inside the baseline when hitting your approach shot, shorten your backswing for better accuracy and consistency, and then accelerate the racket into the ball.

Once you have hit your approach shot, move toward the net in the direction of your shot. But where should you stand to volley? This is a topic of much debate and confusion among many tennis players. The answer is simple. Proper volleying position is not quite halfway from the service line to the net, barely closer to the service line than to the net.

Most players stand either too close to the net or too far away. If you stand too close, you have less time to react and are vulnerable to lobs over your head because of the amount of court left open behind you. In fact, a mediocre lob, which would be handled routinely from a proper volleying position, becomes very difficult if you stand too close. If you stand too far away, you'll have all the lobs covered, but you'll leave too much court open in front of you. This makes it easier for your opponent to hit a ball at your feet. When you get a ball at your feet, you have to volley up (defensively), which is clearly less desirable.

Instead, position yourself almost halfway between the service line and the net. This positioning will make it difficult for your opponent to hit balls at your feet, and you'll be able to cover most lobs hit over your head. Don't forget to move your feet!

Most of us know what an intimidating journey volleying is, whether we love it or hate it. You may have adapted your style to either avoid volleys or keep the point going until you get your preferred shot. But volleying actually isn't that bad. The following are key principles to hitting superior volleys. Practice them enough to feel comfortable, and you will find that volleying adds a new world of possibilities to your game.

1. Remember that the ready position is not quite halfway between the service line and the net, slightly closer to the service line than to the net.

2. Use a continental grip so that you don't have to change grips while at the net. In a continental grip, your hand is rotated about halfway between your forehand grip and your backhand grip.

3. Make contact in front of your body with a short down and forward motion, like a karate chop. If there is time, step into your volley. Push your hand forward when making a volley, and the racket head will come with it.

4. Keep your wrist firm.

5. Hit your volleys with underspin to help give you feel and control.

Keep your arms in front of the body and think "racket position" first, then "move to the ball." Move forward to hit a high floating shot from your opponent. Then return to your original position. See chapter 1 for ideas on when to change your volley position.

Keeping Your Wrist Firm

When you are volleying, you should have a solid grip on your racket and lock your wrist so that it doesn't move throughout your shot. Your wrist should never change position. The racket head should not be out ahead of your hand.

This principle applies to other shots as well. If you are inconsistent on your ground strokes, you may be using too much wrist. Perhaps you slap at the ball. For a more consistent ground game, use a firm wrist on your shots, and you will be more accurate and steady. You won't be able to hit with quite as much pace, but you'll keep a lot more balls in play.

If you can get the ball back six or seven times in a row, you will probably win the point. You should use no wrist snap on the forehand, backhand, and volley. Conversely, you should use maximum wrist snap on all serves and overhead smashes.

Angled Volleys

In both singles and doubles, when the opportunity is right, the best volley will be one that is well angled, meaning that it lands inside your opponent's service box.

You have the best chance to hit a winning angled volley when you have a high ball to hit—one that is well above the top of the net. Naturally, the closer to the net you can get, the better angle you will have, giving you the best opportunity to hit a winner.

Don't try to angle a volley if you are too deep in your court: You will not be able to get enough angle on your volley, and this will open up your own court for your opponent. If you are not in a good spot in your court with a high ball to angle, volley it back deep, preferably to your opponent's backhand. You will win with that volley almost all the time.

The best way to improve your volley is to spend as much time at the net perfecting these techniques as you spend at the baseline. You'll love what a good volley can do for your game.

The Drop Shot

People over 50 don't run and move as quickly as they once did. This means lobs and drop shots will probably be difficult for your opponents to deal with.

Let's start with the drop shot. You should not attempt it unless you are on or inside your own baseline. To make a successful drop shot, you should put some backspin on the ball, so that it won't bounce toward your opponent as much once it lands. To put backspin on the ball, open your racket face slightly, so that it is partially pointing toward the sky, and move your racket from high to low, cutting down the back of the ball. The ball will travel slowly through the air, so you must be on or inside the baseline for the shot to be effective. The shorter the distance this slow ball has to travel through the air, the less time your opponent has to get to it before it bounces twice.

If you make a good drop shot, be sure to position yourself at least four or five feet inside the baseline. In this position, you can get to the drop shot your opponent will probably try if he or she got to your shot in time.

Suppose you have your opponent well behind the baseline, and you attempt a drop shot. But you hit it too high and too deep, so that your opponent gets to it and hits a winner. Does that mean you used the wrong tactic or the wrong shot? No. It simply means that physically you didn't make the drop shot well enough. In this case, don't abandon the drop shot as a good weapon, but use it sparingly and wisely. If you don't hit the drop shot well, you will bring your opponent closer to you and the net. Not good.

Three techniques will dramatically increase your percentage of successfully executing drop shots. First, only try a drop shot from a good position on the court. This means from "no-man's land" forward. The closer you are to the net, the higher your odds become. Never try a drop shot from behind the baseline. From there, you're simply too far away from the net, making the shot more difficult to execute and giving your opponent too much time to run it down.

Second, remember that it is much easier to hit a drop shot if your opponent's shot doesn't have much pace on it. The faster the ball is hit to you, the more difficult it is to execute a drop shot. Try the shot off a slow-paced ball and your percentage will increase.

Finally, always use underspin to hit a drop shot. Underspin will give you the feel and control you need for this difficult shot. This "touch shot" requires a lot of practice, so be patient.

In what cases should you use the drop shot?

1. To try to win the point outright
2. To bring a reluctant volleyer to the net
3. To tire your opponent

You shouldn't use the drop shot all the time, because your opponent will start looking for it and will get to it often enough to make it a costly play.

Returning the Drop Shot

Oops! Your opponent decides to drop shot you. Now what do you do? Assuming you get to the drop shot, you have two basic options. If your opponent has not gotten four or five feet inside the baseline, you can win the point by dropping your shot short over the net. If your opponent has gotten inside the baseline, then a return straight down the line will be very effective. You don't necessarily have to hit the ball hard, as long as you hit it deep. Your opponent is well inside the baseline, so your deep return will land behind him or her.

Don't hit a crosscourt return if your opponent is inside his or her baseline, because the ball will travel across the front of your opponent's body, making it easier for your opponent to hit the ball. As you run to the drop shot, have your racket out in front of you. A short controlled stroke will work. Disguise and placement are more important than the pace of the shot.

You're over 50, and so is your opponent. Neither of you runs the way you used to. Neither of you reacts the way you used to. So, if you execute a good drop shot, and your opponent manages to barely get it back, use the offensive lob. Chances are your opponent won't be able to recover and get to your lob. The other person will do the running, and you'll win the point! Sounds like fun, doesn't it?

The Lob

The lob is a very useful shot to master. There are two types of lobs: the offensive lob and the defensive lob. We'll look at both types of lobs and then discuss specific strategies to help you use lobs successfully.

Offensive Lob

The offensive lob is a low-trajectory shot that is intended to get over a player's head at the net and get far enough behind the player that he or she can't run back to get it. The offensive lob can discourage net rushers, and it can force your opponent to stand farther away from the net. Because your opponent won't be close to the net, he or she won't be able to volley as aggressively, and you will have an easier time directing the ball to your challenger's feet.

As with the drop shot, the offensive lob will work best when you hit it from on or inside your baseline: The shot won't travel through the air as long, giving you a better chance of getting the ball over your opponent's head more quickly.

When you hit an offensive lob over your opponent's head, follow it into the net. If your opponent returns the ball, it will probably be a weak shot or a defensive lob for you to smash. By rushing the net, you'll be in a position to volley off your opponent's attempted passing shot. This way your opponent can't merely get the ball back to stay in the point. Your competitor will have to try a low-percentage shot or put up a defensive lob.

Defensive Lob

The defensive lob is a ball hit high in the air to give you time to recover from being out of position. It is also a good shot to use when you are pushed well behind your baseline, knowing that you probably can't make a high-percentage ground stroke to stay in the point.

To hit a successful defensive lob, use a full swing into the ball and a long follow-through. The baselines are 78 feet apart, and you're also trying to hit the ball 30 or 40 feet in the air, so take a full swing for better success.

Aim down the middle of your opponent's court, because wherever the ball lands, your opponent will have time to get in position behind the ball to attempt an overhead smash. If you get this lob deep, say three to five feet from your opponent's baseline, there's little chance your opponent can hit a winning smash.

Even if you don't get the high lob as deep as you'd hoped, it's still not an easy ball for many people to put away. By using the defensive lob to get back into play from an awkward position, at least you'll make your opponent have to beat you. You won't lose the point with a low-percentage try.

Using Shots You Don't Like to Receive

Remember our earlier premise, "If you don't like it, your adversary probably doesn't either"? Let's think about that for a moment.

It's very difficult to hit an overhead smash when you have to look up into the sun, right? Then why not lob fairly frequently when your opponent is looking into the sun? Not only will your opponent not be able to smash very well, but your opponent will also have trouble adjusting his or her eyes for the next shot.

You don't like to have to hit a backhand overhead, do you? Neither does your competitor! When you can, try to direct your offensive lob over the backhand side of your opponent. You will most certainly get a weak return, if the ball gets returned at all.

Obviously, you have to know whether your opponent is right-handed or left-handed, or in doubles if one is a lefty. If you are playing a lefty, you must know where that rascal is when you decide to hit your offensive lob. Such details make the difference between winning and losing, particularly if you and your opponents are equal in ability.

Let's look at another way you can use an offensive lob. Let's assume you're playing doubles and both your opponents are back on their baseline. Why not use your offensive lob and follow it to the net? Sound crazy? Think about it. Preferably, you'd hit your low lob to the backhand side of your opponent. It would likely bounce up high on the backhand side, a shot no one likes to have to return.

If you can, aim this lob to the backhand side of the opponent playing the ad court, because unless that player is very alert and quick, the ball will catch him or her on the backhand side. This, of course, assumes the player is right-handed.

If you try the same play on your opponent in the deuce court, unless you hit your low lob very accurately, the ad court player will take the shot on the forehand, defeating the purpose. Like you, your opponents probably hit high forehands better than high backhands.

This type of strategy is fun to try. It may not always work, but it will give your opponents one more thing to worry about. No strategy works all the time. The trick is to mix things up a little.

Mixing It Up

It's true that they say, "If it ain't broke, don't fix it." And it's true that if your initial tactics in a game are helping you to win easily, you might not want to change anything. However, against most opponents, you will be more successful if you vary your tactics. The more tactics and shots you can throw at your opponents, the more your opponents will have to think and adjust.

Oftentimes, a certain shot or tactic may not win the point for you, but it can send your opponents a message for later in the match. For example, on your return of serve in doubles, try to go down your opponents' alleys once in a while. You may lose that point, but you're sending a message to your opponents: "Stay home and watch your alleys, because I can and will hit some returns down there."

As another example, perhaps your opponents are crowding the net too closely. Try to hit an offensive lob over one player's head. Maybe you hit the lob shorter than you wanted, and the other team wins the point. But you have "told" your opponents that if they keep crowding the net, you're going to lob over their heads. Physically, you didn't hit the shot the way you wanted to, but the strategy was good.

These tactics, if done at opportune times and with some thought and planning, can make your opponents wary and cautious. Indecision usually takes aggressiveness out of a tennis player.

You should always strive to play your game, what you do best, and in so doing, force your opponents to respond to what you are doing. This puts them on the defensive and takes their game plans away from them.

Returning the Lob—Using the Smash

Now let's reverse the situation and talk about how to respond to the lob. We'll discuss how to deal with the offensive and defensive lobs, how to handle the sun, and how to recover after the smash.

Returning the Offensive Lob

Let's start with an offensive lob by your opponent. Because it has a low trajectory, you should make every effort to hit the ball in the air, being as aggressive on the smash as possible. If you don't hit the lob in the air, once it lands behind you it will continue to run away from you. You will have a difficult time catching up to it, and, even if you do catch up to it, you will only have one play to make—to hit a high defensive lob back. So try to stay in the point by smashing the offensive lob in the air. Don't try some low-percentage passing shot, and whatever you do, don't try that between-the-legs shot you see the pros make once in a while. Those between-the-leg shots rarely go in. We call them "closet shots" because you should "put 'em in the closet and leave 'em there."

When your opponent hits an offensive lob that you can reach, immediately turn sideways and get your racket up near the back-scratching position, so that you can make contact in front of your body, just as you do when you serve.

Preparing to smash requires different positioning than does preparing to serve. When you serve, you drop your racket down toward the ground, bring it up behind your back, and then make the serve. But on the overhead smash, you should shorten your racket preparation by immediately lifting the racket up and dropping the racket head behind your back, which automatically cocks your wrist.

Be sure to use a maximum wrist snap at impact, and try to hit your smash flat. This will give you maximum speed on the smash. Don't be afraid of the overhead. You are normally hitting it from well inside the baseline, and you have the entire court to smash into. Go for it!

Returning the Defensive Lob

How should you handle a high defensive lob from your opponent? One thing is for sure: Never try to smash it in the air. Always allow the lob to bounce first, even if you're making the smash from close to the net. Your opponent has hit the lob high in order to have time to get back into position to defend against your smash. Your challenger can get into position before you can touch the ball, regardless of when you hit it. The ball will be dropping rapidly, having been hit very high, so it will pass through your hitting zone fairly quickly. But once it bounces up, it will come down more slowly. This will make it easier for you to time the ball and allow you to make a solid smash.

Remember these three things when returning a defensive lob:

1. Always allow the defensive lob to bounce before you hit it.

2. Position yourself well behind the bouncing ball, so that you can shuffle into the smash with all your weight going into your smash, making contact in front of your body.
3. The flatter you hit the smash, the faster it will travel. Less spin always equals more speed. Place yourself sideways, get your racket up into the hitting position, and give it a good whack.

One final thought about the overhead smash: Be aggressive. Unlike the serve, where you are behind the baseline and have to hit the ball into the smaller service area, you now have the entire court to use. In addition, you are probably hitting from inside your baseline, so that you have an even better angle to smash into the opposite court. Don't forget to use a maximum wrist snap. Try to make contact in front of your body as you do when serving, and *go for broke!*

Returning a Lob While Looking Into the Sun

What if you have to smash a lob while looking into the sun? Immediately position your body in relationship to the ball so that you don't have to look directly into the sun. This isn't always easy to do, so, in addition, use your free hand to shade your eyes from the sun. When smashing, you should have your free arm extended upward for balance anyway—some people even point at the ball with the free hand. With your hand up, try to shade your eyes from the sun.

If it's a defensive lob, set yourself in a position to smash it, but if the sun is a problem, allow the lob to bounce and come down so that you can return the shot with your forehand. At least this way you won't be blinded by the sun and make an unnecessary error. If you want to really enjoy a great feeling, line up well behind a defensive lob your opponent has hit, allow it to bounce, then shuffle into your smash, hitting it flat. Just let it rip! What a strong, solid shot you will achieve.

Recovering After a Smash

Recovering into position immediately after an overhead smash is critical in both singles and doubles. When you are hitting an overhead, you are most likely in an offensive position, dictating the point. If you don't hit an outright winner on the shot, you are probably setting yourself up to hit the winner on the next one. But many players spend so long admiring the fantastic overhead they just hit that they forget to get into position for the ball that might come back.

You must prepare for your next shot immediately after hitting the current one. If you don't hustle back into position and maintain your concentration, the beautiful shot you just made may not matter. After your overhead, recover back into position at the net and put the next ball away. Don't give your opponent a free point by not paying attention.

The Backhand

If your wrist is strong enough to hit a powerful forehand, why isn't it strong enough to hit a hard backhand? It's all in the grip.

The Backhand Grip

When you hit the forehand with an Eastern, or shake-hands grip, the hand is behind the grip. It is in a strong position to counteract the impact of the ball. If you attempt to hit the backhand without changing your grip, all you have behind the racket to counteract the impact are your fingertips. A very weak grip produces a very weak backhand.

Try to change from the forehand grip to the backhand grip by moving your hand about a quarter of a turn over the top of the racket handle. The big knuckle of your index finger should be over the first upper bevel of the handle. By changing your grip like this, you will get the meaty part of your hand below the thumb behind the grip for more resistance as the ball hits the racket.

Pantomime the backhand without a racket. The back *edge* of your hand should be pointing toward your opponent, but the *back* of your hand should be pointing toward the sky, not toward your opponent. You will have more power with this grip because your wrist won't buckle as it might if the back of your hand were leading the racket through the shot.

Your free hand on the throat of the racket can help you change grips. Between shots relax your grip, and let the free hand turn the racket from the forehand grip to the backhand grip or the other way around. Change grips as you prepare for the shot. If you have time to take your racket from the ready position to the hitting position on forehand or backhand, you have time to change your grip.

One-Handed Backhand

If you hit your backhand one-handed, you have two shot options. First, with the racket head above the contact point, slice down and forward, imparting backspin or slice. The ball will not travel as fast as a flat or a topspin shot, but it can be effective for a baseline rally. Once the slice bounces, it will stay lower and can be more difficult for your opponent to handle. However, the trajectory of a sliced backhand is more in a straight line, and sometimes it even will rise in flight. If you hit it fairly hard, the ball will barely clear the net. It won't dip unless hit very softly (a dink shot). If your opponent is at the net, the sliced backhand will probably be easier for him or her to volley because it will be above the top of the net.

The second option is to prepare behind or just below the contact point with the racket head perpendicular to the ground. Swing forward from low to high and you will automatically impart topspin. You are hitting a round object with an upward glance, so that the object, in this case the ball, will tumble forward (topspin). This type of shot can be hit harder because of the topspin which will give you safety over the net. The topspin will help bring the ball down in your opponent's court. The ball can clear the net by three or four feet. If you want to hit the ball deep, you must hit it high enough that it clears the net by at least three or four feet.

If your opponent is at the net, try to hit the topspin closer to the top of the net. The spin will make the ball dip low, which will make your opponent volley up from a defensive position. Because your opponent will have to worry about getting the ball up over the net and still keep it in the court, he or she won't be able to hit it too hard. A moderate topspin will be a great weapon in your tennis arsenal. You don't have to roll your hand over to hit topspin, and you don't have to brush up the back of the ball to impart topspin. Prepare slightly below the contact point and finish high. Presto! You have topspin.

Two-Handed Backhand

Many players hit the backhand using two hands. Some choose not to change grips and simply add the other hand to gain power to counteract the force of the ball. But the best players using two-handed backhands roll the bottom hand over the top of the grip as suggested for the one-handed backhand.

The fundamentals for a two-handed backhand are the same as for a one-handed backhand: early preparation, good shoulder turn, and contact out in front of the body. The racket head should follow down the line of the intended path of the shot and finish over the shoulder of the racket arm.

To hit with pace, remember to hit as if the racket is an airplane taking off from a runway and not a helicopter going straight up. If you come straight up behind the ball, you will impart excessive topspin but produce very little pace, and the ball will dip quickly and either land short in your opponent's court or go into the net.

A two-handed backhand offers these advantages:

- A good solid grip on the racket will give you more power because the racket head will stay firm at impact.
- You can deceive your opponent by waiting until the last possible moment and then whipping the ball crosscourt by snapping the upper hand to move the racket head earlier.

On the other hand, you cannot reach as far when you hold the racket with both hands, so you will need to be quicker about the court to get set up for the shot. This will require more running. The low angled shot is difficult to play for the two-hander.

As a player over 50, consider the trade-offs of the two-handed backhand. If you need increased speed and power on

DOROTHY "DODO" BUNDY CHENEY

Citizenship: United States of America

Best known for: Winning the most titles in the USTA (301)—more than any other man or woman

If you're a tennis fan, the name Dodo Cheney is synonymous with tennis! Dodo came from a family of great tennis players. Her father won the US Doubles Championships three times and her mother, May Sutton Bundy, won at Wimbledon.

Dodo has always had a flowing style, with a reliable backhand and a powerful forehand. She was accurate with her ground strokes and an overall very intelligent player.

She has played tennis nearly all of her life and has won well over 300 USTA National titles. I can't think of anyone who loves to play the game of tennis more than Dodo Cheney.

Accomplishments

Won the Australian singles title in 1938

—Tony Trabert

the backhand, the two-handed grip will help your game. But if you want to minimize running, the one-handed backhand might be the technique for you.

Footwork

Proper footwork is essential to setting yourself up for a solid return. Assess the shot your opponent is going to make, and position yourself to be in the middle of your opponent's possibilities. Get to a spot where you'll be able to cover either side in the same distance. Good balance and quick footwork will make you a tough opponent.

Ready Position

In the ready position, stand with your feet about shoulder width apart. Bend slightly at the waist and slightly bend the knees. This puts your body weight on the balls of your feet, so that you are in a good position to move in any direction.

Moving to the Ball

If the ball coming to you is going to land fairly close to you, try to shuffle sideways (sidestep) to get to the side of the ball. Plant your back foot and step into your shot. Then shuffle back into position to wait for the next shot.

If you have to run for a wider ball, take longer running steps to get in the vicinity of the ball, and then make small adjusting steps to get into the ideal hitting position. Try to arrive with your weight on your back foot, so that you can step into your shot.

Assuming you are right-handed and you are taken out wide to the right by your opponent, your last step should be with your right foot. Plant the right foot and rotate your shoulders as you hit the forehand. Push off the right foot to come back into the center of the court. If, instead, you finish on your left foot or front leg, your body will be in your way as you attempt the forehand. Your back will be toward the middle of your court, and you will have to turn all the way around to run back into position.

When you run wide to the backhand side, you should plant your right (front) foot to make your shot. Your body will not restrict your swing because your shoulder is in front. If you run wide and plant your left foot, you won't be able to coil your shoulders, which you must do for an effective backhand shot.

The Split Step

The split step is the key to achieving good balance and sound movement for the next shot. Use the split step when serving, volleying, and at any time approaching the net. The split step is a small hopstep, as in hopscotch, that places weight evenly on the balls of both feet. Jump an inch or two off the ground and land on the balls of your feet, landing on both feet at the same time, with your feet about shoulder width apart and your knees slightly bent.

Split step.

Use this hopstep or hesitation no matter where you are on the court as soon as your opponent begins to swing forward into the ball. The split step allows you to move comfortably in either direction. If you try to run without split stepping, you will be unable to adjust quickly to move right or left.

When you learn to time this move and execute it properly, you will react with greater ease to the ball even if you are not in the best position on the court. Split step and you should avoid split sets!

Final Thoughts

As your game matures, develop your weaker shots and continue to improve your stronger ones. You can also analyze your opponents' weaknesses and strengths to help you choose which shots will be most effective in a particular match. Let your footwork and stroke analysis give you the advantage.

Conditioning for a Stronger Game

If you get your body in shape before you go out on the court, you'll play better tennis and have fewer injuries.

Many factors affect your ability to play tennis for a lifetime. Having adequate strength, endurance, and flexibility can help you use proper stroke techniques, hit the ball with good pace and direction, and prevent injuries. Likewise, warming up and cooling down can improve your performance and limit injuries and soreness. All of these issues relate to conditioning, which can make tennis not only more enjoyable, but also safe for a lifetime.

If you are not able to perform your tennis strokes properly or get into position quickly enough, you may be lacking one or more of the undergirding physical elements—muscular strength and endurance, cardiovascular endurance, and flexibility. For example, perhaps you hit your ground strokes and serve great at the start of the match. But as the match progresses, you start making errors, your strokes break down, and you come up a step short on getting to balls. It could be that the mechanics of your stroke break down because you lack one or more of the undergirding physical elements. If you improve your muscular strength and endurance, cardiovascular endurance, and flexibility, you will be able to sustain the level of play with which you began the first set.

Conditioning Definitions

Let's consider some definitions related to conditioning.

• **Muscular strength:** Muscular strength is the maximum amount of force that a muscle or group of muscles can produce when moving a body part. Muscular force is crucial to developing power in your overall tennis game. The more power you have, the more speed you'll generate on the ball and the quicker movements you'll make on the court.

• **Muscular endurance:** Muscular endurance is the ability of muscles or groups of muscles to produce force repeatedly and constantly over an extended period of time. In tennis, muscular endurance allows you to be able to hit stroke after stroke and repeatedly take several quick steps needed in a rally.

• **Cardiovascular endurance:** The circulorespiratory system (heart, lungs, arteries, etc.) transports oxygen to the muscles, utilizes the oxygen in the skeletal muscles, and carries away the waste products produced in the muscles. In tasks requiring maximum effort, if the performance lasts longer than one minute, aerobic metabolism occurs. Although most rallies in tennis don't last over a minute and are considered mostly anaerobic, relying primarily on muscular endurance as opposed to cardiovascular endurance, cardiovascular conditioning may help you recover between points, games, and sets.

• **Flexibility:** Flexibility is the range of motion through which a limb or body part moves at a joint. In tennis, flexibility reduces the chances of injury and improves performance. By increasing your range of motion, you can stretch your muscles farther prior to your hit, which can help you produce more force.

Whether you play tennis two to three times a week, have been out with an injury, play tennis once a month, or have merely been thinking about playing tennis, you may want to consider improving your overall conditioning.

Participating in a conditioning program that improves muscular strength and endurance, cardiovascular endurance, and flexibility will enhance your tennis longevity, both in each match and for a lifetime. Proper conditioning will allow you to play with as little pain as possible and hit the ball with more pace while moving more quickly on the court.

If you're playing tennis two or more times a week, you are probably more fit than most people in your age group. Although you may be satisfied with your conditioning level, you can improve your level of play and prevent injury by focusing on conditioning. Research has indicated that many players who play tennis two or more times a week still lack flexibility. So even if you think you don't need to work on other aspects of conditioning, you probably could improve your flexibility, which will give your game more power and reduce your risk of injury.

If you've been out with an injury and are trying to get back into playing again, if you play only once a month, or if you are thinking about taking up tennis, you must seriously consider participating in a good conditioning program. Tennis is very demanding on the body structures. Hitting the ball and making quick stop-and-go movements stresses the body in ways that might be new to it. If you get your body in shape before you go out on the court, you'll play better tennis and have fewer injuries.

Strength Training

Strength training is the use of progressive resistance methods to increase your ability to exert or resist force. On its most basic level, it is the use of lifting weight to increase your muscle strength or endurance. For a muscle to grow stronger or gain endurance, you have to gradually add weight or increase repetitions—this is the "progressive" part. Exercise scientists agree that carefully planned resistance training programs improve body development and sports performance. You can use your own body weight (as in sit-ups and push-ups), tension bands, free weights, and weight machines to achieve your strength training goals. Strength training for tennis players differs from that of other sports. You should consult a strength training professional who is familiar with tennis and can guide you in exercises that are safe and will provide optimal benefits for your tennis game.

Strength training provides many benefits:

1. Increased muscular strength, which adds power to your game and increases the speed of the ball and your movement on the court.

2. Improved motor skills, which in turn improve your ability to make adjustments easily on difficult ball positions. You can develop better balance, agility, and spontaneous movements.

3. Protection against injuries, especially when you are hitting off balance or catching a ball late.

4. Improved self-image and confidence on the tennis court.

5. Protection against injuries by strengthening your support structures, such as tendons, ligaments, and bones.

Although there are benefits to strength training, you must also be aware of the following risks:

1. If you do not train properly and carefully, you can injure yourself while strength training. These injuries can occur suddenly and last a short or long time (e.g., a pulled hamstring or groin muscle) or they can occur over time and have long-lasting effects on joints, ligaments, or muscle tissue (e.g., "tennis elbow").

2. During a strength training session, you might experience increased blood pressure and, if not breathing properly, "weightlifter's blackout."

Every tennis player past 50 should consider the following strength-training guidelines:

1. Before starting a strength-training program, get a thorough physical examination. Let your doctor know what types of exercises you're planning to do. Certain medications can have an adverse effect on your workout. Pain medication may mask or cover up an injured body structure. Talk with your doctor about these issues.

2. If possible, obtain proper supervision by a qualified trainer. Improper technique can cause injury. There is a right way and a wrong way to train. Because strength training for tennis is different from strength training for other sports, seek a trainer who has knowledge of the game and how to strength train for optimal benefits.

3. Train at least two to three times a week. Rest at least 24 hours between each session.

4. To gain strength, progressively increase, over time, the resistance or weight that you are working with.

5. Tennis calls upon almost all the major muscles in the body, from the feet up through the arms and hands.

Design your strength-training program to work the major muscle groups, including your quads, hamstrings, calves, abdominals and lower back area, the shoulder area (including your rotator cuffs), chest area, and upper and lower arms.

6. Train both your dominant and nondominant body areas. For example, if you are a right-handed player, your right arm is the dominant arm and the left arm is considered the nondominant arm. Be sure to train both equally.

7. Train the muscles on each side of the joints to help maintain a balanced body and decrease chances of pulled muscles. For instance, if you do an exercise for your quadriceps, be sure to do one for your hamstrings.

8. Work your large muscle groups first and then your smaller muscle groups. You might exercise your quads and hamstrings first and your forearms last.

9. Perform multiple-joint exercises before you isolate single joints. For example, do squats before doing knee extensions, or do bench presses before doing elbow extensions.

10. Concentrate on moving the body part through its full range of motion while using proper technique.

11. Warm up prior to your strength training session. You may use light resistance and perform an easy set. Or you might jog, jump rope, or do some other activity for a few minutes to increase your body temperature.

12. After your strength training session, cool down with flexibility or stretching exercises.

13. The greater the resistance or effort, the longer the rest you should take between each exercise or set of repetitions. You may want to start with 10 to 15 reps per set and do 2 to 3 sets per exercise.

14. Keep a daily log of your workout to track your improvement and record your personal experiences. This will help you decide when you need to change your strength-training program. If your performance decreases or you are no longer improving, you might be bored or overtraining. You may need to adjust your program to boost your

progress. Try changing the amount of resistance (weight), the rest interval, the exercises you are doing, or the number of sets and reps (volume). If you adjust properly, you will soon start making progress again.

15. You may need a longer recovery time or rest interval between your resistance exercises compared to the rest periods you took when you were younger. And, you may need to take a longer rest period than might someone younger who is doing the same workout, especially if the workout is strenuous. Make sure you adjust according to your needs.

Muscular Endurance Training

In tennis, muscular endurance works hand in hand with muscular strength to enhance performance and prevent injuries. To develop muscular endurance, use lower resistance (less weight) and increase the number of repetitions. Muscular endurance training, like muscular strength training, should incorporate an "overload principle." That is, over time you should gradually add repetitions and increase weight to increase endurance. As with strength training, you can use your own body weight, tension bands, various weight machines, or free weights to achieve your desired endurance goals. Circuit training is one type of a muscular endurance training program.

What Is a Circuit-Training Program?

A circuit-training program consists of a number of carefully selected exercises arranged in a certain order so that you proceed from one exercise to another with minimal rest. In a muscular endurance circuit-training program, you can progressively develop muscular endurance while also gaining some muscular strength and cardiovascular endurance. How you set up your circuit-training program will determine which physical element is more enhanced.

By using a muscular endurance circuit-training program you can reap these benefits:

1. Improved ability to run down and hit shots time and time again.
2. Improved ability to recover between points, games, and sets.
3. A tremendous workout in a short amount of time. A circuit-training session takes 45 to 60 minutes to complete. This includes a warm-up and cool-down with flexibility exercises. If you have a limited amount of time to work out and play tennis, this is the program for you.

Circuit-Training Guidelines

Follow these guidelines for your circuit-training program:

1. Make sure you warm up for at least five minutes before you start working through the circuit.
2. Make sure the stations for your resistance exercises include exercises that work all the major muscle groups of the lower and upper limbs, back, and abdominal area; exercises that emphasize specific tennis movements, such as your service motion and ground stroke patterns (i.e., use a weighted racket or hand weight and do the actual service motion or use a weighted medicine ball and hold the ball with both hands and swing or turn your torso from one side to the other to help strengthen your abs); and stations that alternate body parts or muscle groups, such as going from upper-body exercise to lower-body exercise to abdominal exercises, and so forth.
3. Consider the time you will spend on each portion of your circuit-training session: Plan your workout to last between 45 and 60 minutes. Take the time to complete 12 to 15 repetitions per exercise. The length of your rest interval between exercises should be similar to the amount of time you rest between points in a tennis match.

4. Follow these resistance guidelines: On each exercise, start with a resistance that is 40 percent of your maximum lift or effort on that exercise. Your maximum effort (called the 1RM in strength-training jargon) is the heaviest amount of weight you can lift on an exercise one time. Find your maximum effort on all the resistance exercises before you start your circuit-training program so that you will know what resistance to start with. Increase the amount of resistance (weight) when you are able to complete 15 repetitions in 30 seconds on your last set. A set is one series of 12 to 15 repetitions done without resting. In a circuit-training program, you will do three sets per exercise.

5. Do three laps with about 10 to 15 stations. You have completed one lap when you have used all the stations one time and have completed one set of each exercise at each station. If you do three laps of 15 stations, you should be able to complete the session within 60 minutes.

6. Do some flexibility exercises after you have completed the circuit-training session.

A Circuit-Training Program on the Tennis Court

If you do not have access to a fitness facility or prefer to be out on the court, try this on-court circuit-training program (see the illustration on page 80). All you need are some light dumbbells, a small exercise mat, and a section of two-by-four (for toe raises). You can use tension bands in place of dumbbells. The format for the on-court program is similar to the circuit-training program in a fitness facility, except that you stay at each station for only 30 seconds, or 12 to 15 repetitions, before you move to the next station. Some of stations at the fitness facility example have two exercises you can do on the machine before you move to the next station, whereas on the tennis court you are only doing one exercise per station so you would move to the next station after you have completed 12 to 15 reps. You can add more stations as desired and use your own body weight, tension bands, dumbbells, or barbells for resistance. You can do the workout yourself, with a partner, or with a group of people.

On-court circuit-training program

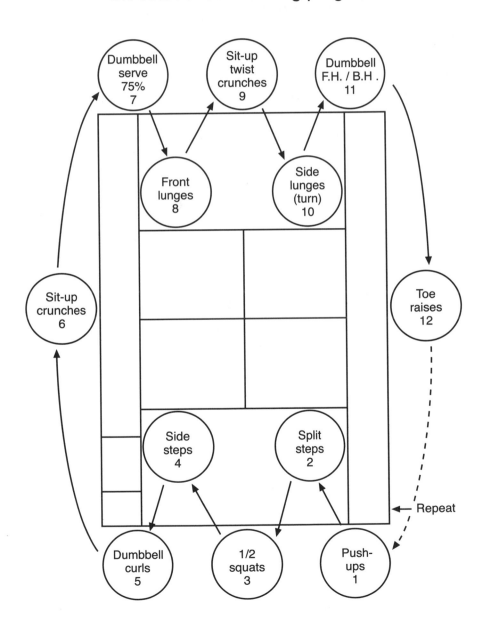

Varying and Monitoring Your Circuit Training

You can increase, decrease, or change stations, time, resistance, and laps based on your specific training goals. For example, if you want to improve your aerobic capacity, add stations such as jumping rope and jogging on a treadmill. If you want to increase your muscular strength, increase your resistance and do fewer repetitions.

Monitor your heart rate to gauge your endurance training and to stay within a safe training intensity. After completing each lap, take your pulse for six seconds and add a zero to the count. This is your heart rate in beats per minute. A standard training target heart rate is 70 to 80 percent of your maximum heart rate (i.e., 220 minus your age). For example, if you are 55 years old, your maximum heart rate is 165 beats per minute (220 minus 55). Your target heart rate for your training session, then, is 115 to 132 beats per minute (or 165 times 0.7 and 0.8, respectively).

Consider playing upbeat music to make your workout fun! Invite your friends to join you. A circuit-training program is ideal for groups of people, because everyone can be at a different station and rotate from one station to the next.

If you find yourself getting bored or your conditioning seems to be leveling out, try a variation of the circuit-training program. You can use the same stations but break the large lap into "mini laps." For example, do the first four stations three times, then move to the next four stations and do them three times, and so on. You can also replace some stations with different exercises. Consider using exercises related to the actual motions of tennis, such as performing the service motion using a dumbbell or tension bands. If you are going to do actual stroke motions with resistance, make sure you perform the motions at no less than 75 percent of the actual stroke speed. This will help prevent injury, preserve your timing, and maintain the neurological pattern of muscular contractions.

The body and your muscles adapt to the specific demands that are placed on them. If you train for strength with high loads, few repetitions, and full recovery periods, you will gain strength. If you train for muscular endurance with low loads, many repetitions, and short rest periods, you will gain muscular endurance. However, keep in mind that using too heavy a weight may throw off the proper timing of your stroke pattern. Set a goal, continually evaluate your progress, and make changes or add variety as necessary.

Cardiovascular Endurance Training

Although tennis is more anaerobic (i.e., activity lasting less than a minute) than aerobic (i.e., activity lasting more than a minute), tennis involves a lot of quick stop-and-go movements performed time and again with brief intervals of rest. In short, tennis requires cardiovascular endurance.

You can incorporate cardiovascular endurance training into your circuit-training program or add interval training to your workouts. To incorporate cardiovascular endurance into your circuit training, include aerobic stations, such as jumping rope or jogging on a treadmill, and decrease your rest interval between stations.

After you have increased your aerobic fitness over the long term by such activities as running, cycling, or aerobic dance, you might add interval training to your workout. In interval training, you do some form of aerobic activity at as high an intensity as you can for intervals ranging from 30 seconds to 5 minutes, with an approximately equal amount of rest between each exercise bout. You might bike, run, jog on a treadmill, use an elliptical trainer, or jump rope. If you have bad knees, hips, or feet, you can safely use such equipment as an exercise bike or elliptical trainer for your interval training. This type of equipment puts less stress on your joints, yet allows you to gain cardiovascular endurance.

You will benefit in two main ways from interval training:

1. Your heart, circulatory system, and lungs will become more efficient in providing oxygen to the muscles of the

body, utilizing the oxygen in the muscles, and getting rid of the waste products produced in the muscles.

2. You will be able to recover faster after a long rally, game, set, or match.

When designing an interval training program, follow these guidelines:

1. Concentrate more on volume than on the intensity of work performed. Start off slow, and build your volume of work. For example, you might start with a 10-minute workout and gradually progress to a 30- or 45-minute workout. You may include a variety of interval training times and rest/recovery times, both ranging from 30 seconds to 2 minutes, in your total interval training program.

2. Determine the intensity of your workout from your heart rate (measured by taking your pulse). Some suggest that the heart rate during interval training should be 150 beats per minute for people 50 to 59 years old and 140 beats per minute for people 60 to 69 years old. Because everyone's fitness level is different, you may want to use a percentage of your maximum heart rate to determine your training heart rate. Remember, your maximum heart rate is 220 minus your age. If you are not in very good aerobic shape, you may want to start your interval training at 70 to 75 percent of your maximum heart rate. If you have been doing some type of conditioning for a long period of time, you may want to start your interval training at 75 to 85 percent of your maximum heart rate. If you have been doing a lot of intense aerobic exercise, such as running, for a long period of time, then you may want to start your interval training at 85 to 90 percent of your maximum heart rate.

3. You must correctly time your rest periods between your workout intervals for cardiovascular training to occur. Use your heart rate to determine when you have recovered enough to start the next workout interval. Experts suggest that you can begin your next workout interval when your heart rate has dropped to 115 beats per minute for those 50 to 59 years old and 105 beats per minute for those 60 to 69 years old. If you are between 70 and 89 years old, rest until your heart is beating approximately 101 beats per minute.

GARDNER MULLOY

Citizenship: United States of America
Best known for: Winning 4 US Doubles
Championships with Bill Talbert

Gardner Mulloy made tennis look easy. He moved fluidly about the court, serving and volleying at every opportunity. His net play was sound and his forehand volley was a tremendous weapon. His smash was flawless and thus always reliable.

His ground strokes enabled him to rally effectively from the baseline and his forehand was his real "concluder." He could hit a winner off that side from anywhere in the court.

Gar has always been physically fit and remains so today and he's still winning (most recently the National titles)—in his late 80s!

Gardner Mulloy was inducted into the International Tennis Hall of Fame in 1972.

Accomplishments

5 Grand Slam titles (5 doubles)
Wimbledon (1 double)
US Open (4 doubles)

—Tony Trabert

4. The rest period should be equal to or less than the workout interval. For example, if you are doing two-minute workout intervals, you should rest for approximately two minutes between each exercise bout, keeping your heart rate at the desired resting rate for your age.

5. Include some flexibility or stretching exercises in your cool-down.

You can use interval training to get past a plateau in your fitness level and to add variety to your workouts. By varying your training methods, you are changing the stimulus, allowing your muscles and body structures to continue to adapt and increase in fitness.

If you enjoy working out on the court rather than off court, you can design an on-court interval training workout. You can even incorporate stroke pattern drills on the court. Start by hitting and moving for at least 30 seconds. Check your heart rate to see if you are reaching your training heart rate. Rest for 20 to 30 seconds, and then do another workout interval of hitting and moving. Continue this rotation of workout and rest until you have completed at least five stroke pattern drills such as crosscourt, down the line, serve and volley, volley, and overhead shots. If you are out of shape, start with fewer drills, hit for only 15 seconds, and rest a bit longer than 30 seconds. As your fitness improves, increase the number of drills and the length of the hitting interval. Decrease your rest interval, but not to less than 30 seconds. If you use your imagination and vary your workouts, you will start to see dramatic changes in your cardiovascular fitness level.

Flexibility Training

Flexibility is specific to each joint and is related to the daily demands placed on the joint structures. That is, only the parts of your body that you stretch will become more flexible. The bony structure of the joint and the soft tissues surrounding the joint can limit the flexibility of the joint. Flexibility and strength are independent of each other. You can be strong yet lack flexibility. As you grow older, your flexibility decreases. Thus, it is important to stay active and to train for flexibility with some consistency.

Participating in a flexibility program can

1. reduce your chances of muscle injury,
2. improve your tennis performance, and
3. provide long-lasting effects of up to eight weeks.

Warm-Up Considerations

People often confuse warming up with stretching. Even though a warm-up often includes stretching, the two are very distinct. You should always warm up before stretching, working out, or playing tennis. Follow these guidelines for an effective warm-up:

1. Warm up before you stretch. A good warm-up raises the total body temperature as well as the core temperature of the muscles, tendons, and ligaments. Many researchers believe that to avoid injury, a person should stretch only after an adequate warm-up.
2. Start with general warm-up activities that involve movement of the major muscle groups of the arms, torso, and legs.
3. General warm-up activities can include jogging, cycling, jumping rope, jumping jacks, and so forth.
4. Then do a specific warm-up with movements and skills that are specific to tennis. Do some split steps with a racket in your hand, and slide to one side or the other as you make an easy forehand or backhand stroke. Try some easy service motions. The specific warm-up increases the temperature in muscles and joint structures and improves the neural responses required in tennis.
5. Continue to warm up until you break out in a sweat.

Either once you have warmed up or after you have completed your entire tennis session, do some stretches to gain flexibility. There are two major types of flexibility training: static and dynamic.

Static or Slow Stretching

You are likely familiar with static stretching. In static stretching you slowly stretch as far as you can and hold the position for 20 to 60 seconds. You should slowly move your body to the desired stretch position and stop to hold the position when you start to feel some minor discomfort. This discomfort should diminish as you hold your position. If you continue to feel discomfort, reduce your stretch position and don't stretch as far next time.

The following photos show some basic static stretches. Although the photos show one side of the body being stretched, you should also stretch the opposite side of your body. For example, after you stretch the right shoulder area, do the same stretch with the left shoulder area.

Shoulder Stretch

Flex one arm across the body. Grasp the elbow with the other hand. Pull the elbow across the body until you feel the stretch.

Shoulder stretch.

Hold the stretch up to a minute and repeat with the other arm. Raise one arm overhead and flex back so your hand touches the shoulder blade. Grasp the elbow with the other hand and steadily pull the elbow backward. Hold the stretch up to a minute and repeat with the other arm.

Chest Stretch

Grab the fence post with your arm extended back and lean slightly forward until you feel some stretch in the chest area. Repeat with the other arm. Hold for one minute.

Chest stretch.

Upper back stretch.

Upper Back Stretch

Grip a fence or net post with both hands. Let your back curve as you pull with your hands. Hold the stretch up to a minute.

Forearm Stretch

Extend one arm, palm up, in front of the body. With the other hand, grasp the fingers of the extended hand. Pull back toward the body. Hold the stretch up to a minute and repeat with the other arm. Extend one arm, palm down, in front of the body.

With the other hand, grasp the back of the extended hand. Pull back toward the body.

Hold the stretch up to a minute and repeat with the other arm.

Forearm stretch.

Lower-Back and Leg Stretch

Sit with one leg extended straight ahead. Flex your other leg and place your foot over the straight leg. Turn your shoulder and place your arm on the outside of the flexed leg. Sit on the floor or court with legs straight ahead. Flex one knee. Stretch your hands down the extended leg as far as you can reach. Grasp the ankle and pull the body toward the extended leg. Hold the stretch up to a minute. Repeat with the other leg extended.

Lower-back and leg stretch.

Upper Quads Stretch

Hold on to a net post for balance. Raise one foot to the rear. Grasp the foot with your hand on the same side. Steadily pull the heel toward the buttocks until you feel the stretch. Hold the stretch up to a minute. Repeat with the other leg.

Calf Stretch

Place your hands against a fence or wall and step back with one leg extended. Keep the heel of your back foot on the ground and lean into the fence until you feel the stretch. Hold the stretch for one minute. Repeat with other leg.

Upper quads stretch.   Calf stretch.

Dynamic Stretching

Dynamic stretching is not as common as static stretching. You may experience muscle soreness for a short period of time when you first start using it. It also requires more balance and coordination than static stretching does. In dynamic stretching, you work to improve the flexibility of sport-specific movements. For tennis, this can consist of exercises related to various tennis skills, but it especially applies to movement on the court. Some experts believe that dynamic flexibility training improves sport-specific movements needed during practice or competition.

You may want to try some of the following dynamic stretches. Keep in mind that dynamic stretching is not for everyone. If you have knee or hip joint problems, avoid the dynamic leg stretches. **Do not do dynamic stretches unless you have been doing static stretches for several months.**

Warm up first, and then start off slowly by doing only one or two of the stretches in your first session. You can do these exercises anywhere—even on the tennis court, walking from one sideline to the other.

Lunge Walk

1. Grip a towel at each end with the hands, and put the towel behind your head.

2. Step forward with one foot and drop into a lunge position. Don't let the front knee go past your foot. Keep your head up and arch your back slightly. The knee of your back leg should be just off the ground.

3. Pause for a brief moment in the bottom position and then repeat with the opposite leg, progressing toward the opposite sideline of the tennis court.

Lunge walk.

Walking Side Lunge

Grip a towel at each end with the hands. Facing the net, take a long lateral (sideways) step with your left foot. Keeping the right leg straight, sink your hips back and to the left. Don't let your left knee go past your left foot. Keep your head up and slightly arch your back. Stand up by bringing your right foot next to your left foot, and repeat the walking side lunge until you have reached the sideline.

Walking side lunge.

Then repeat the side lunge, taking a lateral step with your right foot, so that you go back to where you started.

Walking Knee Tuck

Step straight ahead with the left leg, and as you bring the right leg forward use your hands to pull the right knee up and toward your chest. Pause for a moment. Then step forward with your right leg, and as you bring the left leg forward use your hands to pull the left knee up and toward your chest. Repeat this sequence until you have reached the other sideline.

Walking knee tuck.

Walking High Knee/Opposite Arm Swing

Lift your left knee as high as possible, while swinging your right arm forward with the left leg. Pause a moment, then step down on your left foot. Repeat with the opposite leg and arm movement.

Torso Twists

Grip a towel or racket at each end with the hands . Raise your arms in front of your body so that the arms are parallel to the ground. Slowly rotate your torso to the right and hold the position for a moment. Then slowly rotate your torso to the left and hold the position for a moment. Repeat the torso twists until you have completed 12 to15 repetitions.

Walking high knee/opposite arm swing.

Torso twists.

Stretching

As we grow older, our bodies become less flexible. But if you set up a flexibility training program, you can actually reverse the loss and gain flexibility. Remember, flexibility is specific to each joint. Only the parts of your body that you stretch will become more flexible. Before playing tennis, warm up and do some stretches. After your practice or match, stretch again. When stretching, do not hurry. Take your time and move slowly from one stretch to another. Following this routine will enhance your playing and reduce muscle injuries and soreness.

Recovering After Play

Our discussion of conditioning would not be complete without considering how to recover after a tough practice or match. We recommend that you take the following steps to prevent long-lasting physical injuries:

1. Stretch out within 10 minutes of completing play. This helps relax your muscles and prevents muscle stiffness, which can lead to soreness and injury.

2. Take a shower and change clothes. This will cool your body and help you feel refreshed for your next match.

3. Drink fluids, eat a meal high in complex carbohydrates (bread, pasta) within 30 to 60 minutes after your match, and eat foods high in potassium (fruit, vegetables, potatoes).

4. If you have an injury, ice it for 10 to 15 minutes, two to three times after play to reduce pain, swelling, and inflammation.

5. Do not take an anti-inflammatory or other pain relief substance prior to play. These drugs mask pain and may lead to further damage to the body. However, after play you might you may want to take a safe dosage of anti-inflammatories or pain relief substance to help ease the pain and discomfort.

6. Properly strengthen any body part that has been injured. Pain leads to lack of use, which leads to muscle atrophy. If you incur an injury, start a strengthening program after a period of rest or while playing at a modified pace.

If you take care of yourself by following these simple guidelines, you'll enjoy the sport of tennis for a lifetime!

Final Thoughts

Conditioning for muscular strength and endurance, cardiovascular endurance, and flexibility can improve your game, reduce your chances of injury, and allow you to play pain-free. Tennis is a lifetime sport, and you can increase that lifetime with extra conditioning. Base your conditioning program on your tennis-playing goals. For example, is your goal to be social or competitive? Is it to play once a week or two or more times per week? You can adjust your conditioning program to suit your situation.

The up side to participating in a conditioning program is that you will see an improvement in whatever undergirding physical elements you work on. The down side is that to stay at the level of fitness you have reached, you must continue doing your conditioning program with consistency. The old adage is true: If you don't use it, you will lose it!

Eating for Competition

Hydration! Hydration! Proper hydration is key to success on the tennis court.

Proper nutrition can help you not only perform at your highest level, but also maintain that level as long as possible. Your nutritional intake should match your conditioning and performance goals. Most tennis players have many questions about nutrition. How many calories and how much protein is needed when you are training or playing a tough match? How much carbohydrate should you consume? How much fluid should you drink to achieve proper hydration? Does proper diet prevent muscle cramps? In this chapter we will answer these questions and more.

First we need to clarify that the word *diet* in this chapter does not mean a plan to lose weight. Instead, by *diet* we mean your daily nutritional intake—that is, what you eat and drink on a daily basis or as you prepare for and recover from a practice or match.

To find out what diet is best for you, consider consulting with a professional nutritionist or dietitian, who can perform a complete diet analysis. You may also use trial-and-error techniques to find which diet or nutrition program works well for you. There are as many good diets as there are tennis players. Body size, intensity of training or playing, age, and sex all can impact your choice of diet. The information in this chapter will help you develop a diet that best suits you.

Setting Nutrition Goals

Before embarking on a particular diet, you should establish your nutrition goals. Goals for an optimal training diet might include the following:

1. To provide basic caloric and nutrient requirements
2. To incorporate nutritional practices that promote good health

3. To achieve and maintain optimal body composition and playing weight

4. To promote physiological adaptations and recovery from training sessions

5. To try variations of precompetition and competition fuel and fluid intake to determine bodily responses

Caloric Intake Per Day

Your level of daily activity, including how much tennis you play, dictates how many calories you should consume. Everyone needs sufficient calories to support daily needs. If you are training and playing tennis, you need to take in additional calories to sustain these extra activities. Your optimal caloric intake may also depend on your body size and the intensity, duration, and frequency of your training or tennis competition. Be sure that the calories you ingest contain a combination of the six essential nutrients recommended by the U.S. Department of Agriculture.

If you want to maintain your weight as you are training or playing tennis on a regular basis, calculate your average caloric intake in the following manner:

1. Divide your body weight by 2.2.

2. Multiply the result of your calculation in step 1 by 30 to 50. Use 30 if you train or play occasionally and at a low intensity. Use a number closer to 50 if you train or play frequently and intensely.

For example, if you weighed 175 pounds, you would divide your weight by 2.2, giving you 79.5. Then you would multiply 79.5 by 30 and 50 to get a caloric range of approximately 2,400 to 4,000 calories. This tells you that you would take in 2,400 calories when you are training at an easy to moderate level of intensity and 4,000 calories when you are training at a high level of intensity.

Six Essential Nutrients

The calories you take in should include all six essential nutrients recommended by the U.S. Department of Agriculture: carbohydrate, protein, fat, vitamins, minerals, and fluids. By understanding the roles of these nutrients and what foods provide them, you can make better decisions about your diet for training and competition.

Carbohydrate

Carbohydrate provides the primary fuel for your muscles when they are working. Carbohydrate is stored in your muscles and liver as glycogen. When your muscles are depleted of glycogen, you experience fatigue and sluggishness, and this limits your ability to play effectively. To maintain energy and stamina, you must ingest enough carbohydrate:

- The higher the intensity of your training or playing, the more important glycogen is as a fuel.
- Your body can store only limited amounts of carbohydrate. Training increases the ability to store carbohydrate and spare protein.

How much carbohydrate should you eat? If you are training at a high intensity, you may increase your intake of carbohydrate to 70 to 80 percent of your daily caloric intake. If you are training at a low or moderate intensity, then 55 to 65 percent of your daily calories should be carbohydrate.

Are there different types of carbohydrate? Yes! Complex carbohydrates (e.g., vegetables, whole grain cereals and breads, fruits, beans, pasta, rice, and lentils) provide a gradual release of glucose, which aids in sustained exercise. Simple carbohydrates (e.g., sugars, syrups, and jellies) are quickly converted into energy that lasts for only a short period of time. Liquid carbohydrate sources are as effective as solid carbohydrates. At times a liquid carbohydrate drink may be more appropriate, especially if you are not hungry after an intense workout on the tennis court. The liquid carbohydrate drink provides you with the needed carbohydrates, and it also helps replace some of the fluids you lost.

Ingesting protein along with carbohydrate within four hours of working out or playing tennis has been shown to significantly increase the rate of glycogen storage. When you shop for a liquid carbohydrate drink, look for one that has protein along with carbohydrate.

Protein

Protein plays a large role in building and repairing body tissue and is necessary in maintaining the immune system. Your body looks to use protein for energy when fewer calories are consumed than are expended. Because protein can only supply up to 5 to 10 percent of the energy needed to sustain prolonged exercise, you may need to increase your total caloric intake if you are very active. If your total caloric intake is insufficient, then you are likely taking in too little protein to both provide enough energy and rebuild your muscles. Use the following calculations to determine approximately how much protein you should ingest for a particular day:

1. Divide your weight by 2.2.
2. Multiply that figure by 0.8 grams if you are doing light to moderate exercise or 1.3 to 1.5 grams if you are doing heavy or intense training or playing.

For example, if you weighed 180 pounds, you would divide your weight by 2.2, which equals 81.8. Then, if you were playing tennis or working out at an easy to moderate level of intensity, you would multiply 81.8 by 0.8 grams to find that you would need approximately 65 grams of protein for that particular day. On the other hand, if your games or workouts were quite intense, you would multiply 81.8 by 1.5 grams and find that you would need 122.7 grams of protein for that day.

Can too much protein in your diet be harmful? If you have preexisting liver or kidney abnormalities, a high-protein diet can lead to further deterioration of function. If you have normal liver and kidney functions, a high-protein diet within some guidelines will probably not cause any problem.

Be sure to heed these precautions if you increase your protein intake:

- Metabolism of protein requires more water than does the metabolism of carbohydrate or fat. If you increase your protein intake, you also need to increase the amount of water you drink.

- Research has shown that sedentary individuals who increase their protein intake excrete more calcium. This suggests a loss in bone density. You don't want to ingest an excessive amount of protein, because it could lead to an accelerated loss of bone density.

More does not necessarily mean better. You should stay within the recommended guidelines. If you are not a vegetarian and are not doing intense training or playing, then your normal diet will probably provide you with enough protein.

Fat

Fat helps the body process certain vitamins (e.g., A, D, E, and K). It also helps protect your organs and provides insulation for your body. Fat is a major source of fuel for exercises of low or moderate intensity, and it is readily available in adequate quantities in most people. Your normal daily intake of fat should be between 20 and 30 percent of your daily caloric intake. No more than 10 percent of the fat you eat should be saturated (e.g., most dairy products, pork, and beef). Eating too little fat can hurt your performance and cause physiological declines. Because fat is the primary source of fuel for low- to moderate-intensity exercise, try not to let your fat level drop below 30 percent of your daily diet when you are doing low- to moderate-intensity endurance training.

Vitamins

Vitamins are organic substances of plant or animal origin that are essential for normal growth, development, metabolic processes, and energy transformations. They also act as catalysts to break down food.

Vitamins Important for Training

These vitamins are particularly important for people who are training:

- Vitamin B_6 helps provides fuel to the muscles by assisting in amino acid (protein) metabolism and the breakdown of glycogen to glucose.
- Vitamin B_1 helps provide fuel to the muscles by assisting in carbohydrate metabolism.
- Vitamin C ensures the healthy formation of connective tissues and helps the body respond to stress.
- Vitamin E decreases muscle loss and damage when you do strength training.

Some evidence suggests that you may need to take in more vitamin C if you are playing tennis or training at a high intensity, especially in a hot climate. In addition, you might need to increase your intake of B-complex vitamins in a hot climate. Finally, if you are playing tennis or training at high altitude, you may need to increase your vitamin E intake.

Vitamin Intake Concerns

Your body does not produce most vitamins—you need to consume them in your diet. However, you need only extremely small amounts of vitamins. Most research has shown that vitamin supplementation does not improve performance if you are already eating an adequate diet with the suggested daily vitamin intake. If you have vitamin deficiencies, supplementing your vitamin intake to normal physiological levels can improve your performance. You can ask a nutritionist or dietitian to conduct a complete nutritional analysis to see whether you are lacking certain vitamins. However, megadoses of vitamins are neither a substitute for vigorous training nor necessary for your body to improve with training. Extremely large doses of vitamins can be toxic, impair performance, and cause health problems. As in other areas of nutrition, more is not necessarily better!

Minerals

Minerals help maintain bone density, energy metabolism, enzyme function, muscle contraction, oxygen transport, insulin regulation, and normal body functions. Microminerals, often called trace elements or trace minerals, are needed in tiny amounts—less than 100 milligrams per day (and often much less). Macrominerals are needed in greater quantities—over 100 milligrams per day.

Microminerals

You might be interested in how these five microminerals are affected by training or playing tennis:

1. **Zinc.** When you are training or playing tennis you may lose a sizable amount of zinc through sweat and urine. However, if your intake of zinc meets the recommended dietary allowance (RDA) you probably don't need to take extra zinc.

2. **Chromium.** The jury is still out on the benefits of chromium on exercise. Some experts have speculated that exercise may increase the requirements for chromium intake. Again, it is best to stay within the RDA.

3. **Copper and selenium.** Although copper may be lost in sweat as you exercise, there is no need to take more copper or selenium than the RDA.

4. **Iron.** Iron deficiency anemia impairs performance. If you have an iron deficiency, taking an iron supplement may improve your iron status and playing performance. Make sure you have been examined and tested for iron deficiency anemia before increasing your iron intake.

Macrominerals

Macrominerals include calcium, chlorine, magnesium, phosphorus, potassium, sodium, and sulfur. Sulfur has no direct effect on training or playing tennis. The other macrominerals listed here are known as electrolytes. When these electrolytes dissolve in body fluids, they produce ions. These ions control the movement of water between fluid compartments, help maintain acid-base balance, and carry electrical current that is important for muscular contraction.

1. **Calcium.** Calcium is necessary for healthy bones and teeth. It is also required for muscle contraction, conduction of nerve impulses, and blood clotting.

2. **Chlorine.** Chlorine plays a role in regulating the pressure of body fluids among different membranes, allowing minerals to be absorbed.

3. **Magnesium.** Magnesium is present in bone and teeth, and it aids in enzyme activity to help nerves and muscles function. You lose magnesium when you sweat, but there is no evidence that supplemental doses improve performance.

4. **Phosphorus.** Phosphorus works with calcium to develop and maintain strong bones and teeth. Phosphorus also helps produce energy for anaerobic activities, such as sprinting to the tennis ball to make your next shot. Several studies have shown that taking more phosphate than normal for several days before competition may improve performance, whereas other studies have shown no beneficial effects. Beware! Phosphorus supplementation over an extended period of time can result in lowered blood calcium levels. It is probably best to stay within the RDA for phosphorus.

5. **Potassium.** Potassium is necessary for muscle contraction and conduction of nerve impulses.

6. **Sodium.** Sodium plays a key role in water balance, conduction of nerve impulses, and muscle contraction. You lose some sodium when you sweat. After exercising, you may want to drink fluids that contain sodium. Sodium appears to help your intestines absorb fluids and may prevent blood plasma from becoming diluted. Increased intestinal absorption stimulates urine production and fluid excretion, which has been inhibited

during exercise. Sodium helps stimulate thirst. If your postexercise beverage has little or no salt, your thirst drive may shut down and you might drink less fluid, causing you to rehydrate more slowly than desired. A word of caution, though: You should never take salt tablets. Such highly concentrated amounts of salt can lead to gastrointestinal discomfort, dehydration, and electrolyte loss.

As with vitamin intake, you should follow the RDA for minerals unless you have been diagnosed with a mineral deficiency. Several multimineral/multivitamin pills are designed with the proper RDAs for seniors. One of these one-a-day pills is usually sufficient. As with vitamins, extremely large doses of minerals can be toxic and may cause health problems.

Water

Water is the most essential nutrient for the body. In fact, you can survive longer without food than without water. Water plays an important role in digestion, circulation, waste removal, building cells, transporting other nutrients, and maintaining normal body temperature. Your blood plasma is primarily water. Blood plasma transports amino acids and glucose to your muscles to help rebuild the muscles and aid in muscle contraction. Fifty to 60 percent of your body weight is water.

When you play tennis or train, your body sweats to help keep cool. As you perspire, your body loses water as well as some electrolytes, so you should replenish your body with water or some type of fluid.

How much water should you drink when you are working out or playing tennis? You have probably heard that you should drink at least eight 8- to 10-ounce glasses of water per day. But everyone is different, and your water needs may vary based on your size and how active you are. If you are not doing intense training or tennis playing, you can follow the general guideline of drinking eight glasses of water a day. To see more specifically how much water you should be drinking, especially on days when you exercise, follow these guidelines from the *Journal of the American Dietetic Association*:

- Multiply your weight by 0.08. This is the minimum number of eight-ounce glasses of water you need on a daily basis. For example, if you weigh 180 pounds you need to drink approximately 14.5 glasses of water per day.
- On days that you work out or play tennis, drink an additional two glasses of water.
- During training or playing tennis, drink four ounces of water every 20 minutes.
- After a workout or match, drink at least two more glasses of water.

Can sports drinks be substituted for water in replacing fluids your body has lost? Although some have claimed that

Drink plenty of fluids in between matches.

electrolytes make sports drinks more palatable and thereby encourage drinking, the available evidence indicates that sodium, as mentioned earlier, is the only electrolyte that is beneficial when consumed during or after.

As you evaluate whether to drink water or a sports drink, you should consider the rate at which an ingested fluid enters your body's water supply. Before fluid can be absorbed into the blood, it must pass through the stomach and into the small intestine. In the small intestine, digestion is completed and nutrients are absorbed into the blood. Two processes affect how fast the fluid will reach your bloodstream:

1. **Gastric emptying.** Gastric emptying is the process by which the fluid leaves your stomach. The higher the caloric content of the fluids you drink, the slower the rate of gastric emptying. You should probably drink fluids that are less than 10 percent carbohydrate. Drink small quantities (i.e., four ounces) every 15 to 20 minutes. For optimal body cooling, drink cool fluids.

2. **Intestinal absorption.** Intestinal absorption is the movement of nutrients through the intestinal wall into the blood. Compared with plain water, fluids with glucose and sodium will greatly speed up intestinal fluid absorption. If you are training or playing tennis for one to two hours in hot and humid conditions, you should drink fluids with a carbohydrate concentration of 2.5 to 8 percent and a moderately high sodium content of 30 to 110 mg. If you are training or playing tennis for over two hours in temperate conditions, you should drink a more concentrated carbohydrate solution (6 to 10 percent) with 30 to 110 mg of sodium.

Nutrition Guidelines for Competition

Your diet the day of a competition should not vary much from what you have been eating while training the days before the match. Following the guidelines given earlier in this chapter will ensure that you will take in the proper amounts and types of nutrients needed for strenuous exercise. What you eat a few hours before the match will have very little nutritional value in improving your performance. Make sure you drink plenty of fluids, ingest some complex carbohydrates that you are used to eating, and enjoy. Do not eat foods that you are not used to eating; you may hinder your performance if you eat something that does not agree with you.

Hydration! Hydration! Proper hydration is key to success on the tennis court. Remember, water helps regulate your body temperature, prevents heat exhaustion, and helps transport nutrients and energy to your muscles.

Before Your Match

Drink fluids continually throughout the day of your competition. Do not rely on thirst as an indicator of adequate hydration. You need to drink before you sense that you are thirsty.

In your prematch meal, eat 50 to 100 grams of complex carbohydrates and drink at least 16 to 24 ounces of water. If possible eat your prematch meal three to four hours before your match. Up to one-half hour before your match, you can drink up to 16 ounces of fluid at a time. In the last half-hour before your match, drink very little water, if any.

During Your Match

It is important to drink what you can during your match as well. Drink four ounces of cool water or sports drink (2.5 to 8 percent carbohydrate and 30 to 110 milligrams of sodium) every 15 minutes and especially when you are changing sides. If you are playing a match that lasts longer than 90 minutes, drink a sports beverage that has carbohydrate and electrolytes, especially sodium. Review the previous section in this chapter on water intake. A small portion of some type of fruit, such as a banana or orange, may help restore lost muscle energy. If you are playing in high temperatures or at a high altitude, you may need to drink more fluid than the guidelines given in this chapter.

JIMMY CONNORS

Citizenship: United States of America

Best known for: Winning 5 US Open Championships on clay, grass, and hard surfaces

© Sportschrome

Jimmy Connors was as tenacious on the tennis court as any tennis player I've seen. His ground strokes were hit aggressively, particularly his two-handed backhand. His return of serve was exceptional, taking the ball early and returning it with added pace and good direction.

He had a long career because his game was sound and he never lacked the motivation to perform at a high level every time he stepped onto a tennis court.

Connors was controversial and often annoyed tennis fans with some vulgar behavior and language on the court, but fans found him colorful and intriguing to watch. He was a master at playing the crowd. When Jimmy came on the court, you always knew he would give 100% effort, no matter what.

James Scott Connors was inducted into the International Tennis Hall of Fame in 1998.

Accomplishments

10 Grand Slam titles (8 singles; 2 doubles)
Australian (1 single)
French (1 double)
Wimbledon (2 singles)
US Open (5 singles; 1 double)

—Tony Trabert

After Your Match

You must replace the fluids that you have lost. Weigh yourself, and for every pound you have lost, drink approximately 16 ounces of fluid. To help prevent muscle tissue breakdown, replace your lost fluid within the first half-hour to two hours after your match. Drink a sports beverage that has both carbohydrate and electrolytes in it. Make sure there is sodium in the drink, because sodium will speed intestinal absorption and help maintain your thirst drive for rehydration. Within four hours of your match, eat some protein. You might choose a sports drink that includes protein along with carbohydrate and electrolytes. If you eat a protein bar or some other solid form of protein, make sure you drink plenty of water. Check the color of your urine. The lighter the color of your urine, the more hydrated you are.

Throughout the day of the match (and really all other times if possible) avoid caffeinated beverages. These drinks act as diuretics and cause the body to lose water. You should also avoid salt tablets—they can cause gastrointestinal discomfort, dehydration, and electrolyte loss and may be hazardous to your health.

Muscle Cramps

What role does nutrition play in preventing muscle cramps? Researchers do not know the exact cause of muscle cramps, but possible causes include:

1. **Dehydration.** Your muscles may start to cramp when you are dehydrated.

2. **Electrolyte imbalance.** Sweat loss and dehydration can disrupt the balance between potassium and sodium. This can especially occur if you train or play for over two hours at a high level of intensity. If you have been eating a proper diet, you should have enough potassium and sodium to maintain a proper balance. However, drinking a sports drink with carbohydrate and electrolytes, in-

cluding sodium, soon after your match can help your body rehydrate appropriately.

3. **Mineral deficiency.** Along with potassium and sodium, you need an adequate amount of calcium and magnesium to help the muscles contract and relax. If you are eating a proper daily diet, you should have enough of these minerals to sustain muscle contraction without cramping.

4. **Fatigue.** Fatigue, defined as a decrease in your muscle's ability to contract, leads to reduced ability of your muscles to produce force and absorb energy. Coupled with dehydration and electrolyte imbalance, fatigue can lead to muscle cramps or injury.

5. **Injury.** Often, the muscles surrounding an injured muscle contract tightly and act as a splint to protect the injured tissue. The protective, contracting muscles or joints then may cramp up.

To gain some relief from a muscle cramp try stretching the muscle slowly. Massaging the cramped muscle may improve circulation and help remove metabolic waste products that may be contributing to the muscle's contraction.

To help prevent muscle cramps, drink plenty of water, eat properly, stretch before and after matches, and train properly—don't get sloppy and take undue risk.

Final Thoughts

A proper daily diet will help you perform your best on the court. Your body is like a fine-working machine—for it to operate at and maintain a high level of productivity, you must give it the proper fuel. You should put as much effort into your nutrition as you put into your training, hitting practice, and playing. Every tennis player has different needs and goals. Your sex, age, body size, and training and playing intensity may dictate the type of nutrition that is best for you. Whatever daily diet you choose to follow, reevaluate your diet often and make changes that will best suit your training and playing style.

Winning Strategies for Different Opponents

*Try something other than your favorite shot once in a
while, and your opponent will never be sure where
you plan to hit the ball.*

You've heard the saying, "Different strokes for different folks."
The same is true for tennis. You will often play against people
with different games and different strategies, and you'll have
to know how to respond. In this chapter we'll look specifically
at how to play against the dinker, the hard hitter, the lefty, and
the player with the two-handed backhand.

The Dinker

You have probably run into the dinker—that annoying crea-
ture who gets everything back, but never hits the ball very
hard. If you're not careful, eventually you'll get frustrated and
start to try low-percentage shots, which will make for a lot of
errors. Show me a dinker, and I'll show you someone with a lot
of trophies. Players who run down the ball and keep it in play
are tough to beat.

Your best response to the dinker is to rally with patience,
always looking for a short ball or one floating in the air so that
you can attack your opponent from well inside your baseline.
Normally, an approach shot hit fairly deep into your opponent's
backhand will pay dividends. Or, if you're far enough into your
court and the ball is higher than the top of the net, try an
angled shot. If you can make your shot land in the corner of
your opponent's service box, you should have enough angle to
win the point outright.

Normally, dinkers don't like to come to the net and are not
good volleyers. So another strategy to consider is to rally until
you get a short ball and then to make a drop shot. Either the
shot will win the point outright because your opponent is well
behind the baseline, or the drop shot will bring your opponent
to the net, where the dinker doesn't want to be. Don't try to
make the drop shot perfect. Just make it short enough to bring
that weak-volleying dinker to the net.

An offensive lob can then be effective. But, as with the drop shot, if you attempt a passing shot, you don't need to make it perfect, because the dinker is not normally a good volleyer. Rather than miss your passing shot by trying to play it too close to the line, make the poor volleyer try to beat you by having to volley.

Against the "push baller" you might also try to hit short shots, where your opponent has to come forward to hit a low return from a short, low position on the court. If the subsequent

Ilie Nastase, about to make a backhand volley. Note how his racket head is above the ball and slightly open.

Citizenship: United States of America

Best known for: Being 1 of 5 Centurions, winning at least 100 pro titles overall in singles and doubles

© Hulton–Deutsch Collection/CORBIS

Tall and lanky, Stan Smith had a very dominating serve and followed it into the net where he was a very good volleyer. His long reach made him tough to pass and he dealt with lobs with a powerful and reliable overhead.

He was a stalwart on the US Davis Cup teams for 10 years in both singles and doubles. His finest moment in Davis Cup play was when he won the deciding match to defeat Romania, in Bucharest, before a rough and rowdy crowd. Stan has always been a gentleman and true sportsman.

Stan Smith was inducted into the International Tennis Hall of Fame in 1987.

Accomplishments

7 Grand Slam titles (2 singles; 5 doubles)
Australian (1 double)
Wimbledon (1 single)
US Open (1 single; 4 doubles)

—Tony Trabert

return is not deep into your court, you can do some damage by hitting your next shot deep. Again, keep in mind that the dinker doesn't want to come to the net, so your opponent probably won't follow his or her shot off your short ball to the net. Instead, the dinker will probably try to retreat to a spot behind the baseline and probably can't make it in time to return your deep shot.

If you play fairly aggressively and hit the ball fairly hard, you might try to hit some outright winners off the dinker's second serve. The second serve will probably land short and bounce up fairly high. Position yourself well inside your baseline so that you can attempt your aggressive return by getting the ball at the top of the bounce, giving you the best angle down into your opponent's court.

In this situation you have several options: Hit an angled return, a deep return crosscourt, or a deep return down the line. Hit the shot you do best, because that's your high-percentage play. If you hit your forehand down the line better than you hit it crosscourt, make your play down the line. If your backhand crosscourt is better than your backhand down the line, go crosscourt. Even though your opponent may know what's coming, your best shot from a position well inside your baseline will probably pay off.

Having said this, mixing up your shots when you can will make it even tougher on your opponent. Try something other than your favorite shot once in a while, and your opponent will never be sure where you plan to hit the ball.

The Hard Hitter

Let's talk about the big, hard hitter who is somewhat erratic. The best way to play this kind of player is to be as steady and consistent as you can and to force the big hitter into errors. Incorporate these two tips against the heavy hitter:

1. Don't put a lot of pace on your ball, so that the hard hitter will have to take a bigger swing at the ball to put speed on the shot. Big swings often translate into unforced errors.

2. Try to hit the ball deep, keeping that big hitter well behind the baseline. That way you'll have more time to get to your opponent's shots.

Putting less pace on your shots can bother this hard hitter, but getting the ball very deep is more important. You don't have to hit hard, but you should try to hit deep. Also, try to get some of your shots to bounce high to take away the heavy hitter's effectiveness. It is difficult for anyone to hit a high ball hard and accurately.

You might also try to hit a short ball that will stay low—it's hard to be aggressive from a low position, and this type of opponent probably doesn't know how to tone things down. Sluggers like to hit everything hard, so they are likely to make errors when they are moving forward and hitting the ball from a low position.

If, in your effort to get your shot short and low, you hit a little too high or deep, your opponent may be able to hit a clean winner. That doesn't mean your tactic was wrong. It means you didn't physically execute the shot well enough. Don't be afraid to try the same tactic again. If you execute it well enough, it will probably work. Nothing you try on the tennis court will work every time, but it's always worth trying!

A natural instinct for every tennis player is to try to hit the ball away from the opponent. Against a big hitter, sometimes you're better off hitting the majority of your shots straight down the middle. This will cut down the angles your opponent will have, giving you a better chance to get to those hard-hit shots. If you hit your shot crosscourt, you open up your court to a certain degree, making it more difficult for you to get to the hard-hit ball. If you try an even sharper angle, unless you do it very well, you really open up your court for your opponent.

When you serve against the heavy hitter, try to get a high percentage of your first serves in, even if you have to take some pace off the ball. Let's say your opponent stands on the baseline waiting to return your first serve. You serve a fault. If your opponent is smart, he or she will take at least one step forward to wait for your second serve and will step into the return. This will put your opponent five or six feet into the court, where he or she can take your second serve early and higher on the bounce. This makes it easier for your opponent

Citizenship: Australia

Best known for: Winning the Grand Slam
as an amateur and a pro

© AP Photo

Rod Laver accomplished something no other man or woman has ever done in tennis: He won the Grand Slam in 1962 as an amateur. I personally signed him to a professional contract in 1963, so until Open Tennis came to pass in 1968, he was no longer allowed to play in the Grand Slam tournaments—only amateurs could play. In 1969, the second year of Open Tennis when amateurs and pros could play in the same events including the Grand Slam tournaments, "Rocket" won the Grand Slam again, as a professional, making him the greatest tennis player of all time.

Rod had an all-court game and the little left-hander attacked at every opportunity. He had powerful ground strokes and was able to hit extra top spin off both sides. Rod was a wonderful volleyer with quick reflexes and a solid, reliable smash. He was very quick around the court.

Rod Laver was inducted into the International Tennis Hall of Fame in 1981.

Accomplishments

20 Grand Slam titles (11 singles; 6 doubles; 3 mixed doubles)
Australian (3 singles; 4 doubles)
French (2 singles; 1 doubles; 1 mixed)
Wimbledon (4 singles; 1 doubles; 2 mixed)
US Open (2 singles)

—Tony Trabert

to make a powerful return, and it gives you less time to respond.

By getting your first serve in, your opponent will be standing farther back, and you will have more time to get to the return of serve. You might even try to hit your "cannonball" first serve once in a while to keep your opponent from stepping in on your first serve. If you are not a big server, mix it up. Serve some wide, some down the middle, and some straight at the body. Try not to use a serving pattern that your opponent can catch on to.

The Lefty

Oops! Here comes a left-hander with a tough slice serve. What should you do? Because lefty will probably slice the serve down the middle in the first court, stand a little more to your left than normal.

In the second court, you'd better straddle the singles side-line because lefty will try to ace you wide or get you way out of position with that swinging serve. Move diagonally forward and to your left to cut off the serve before it can take you out of the court. Remember, too, that the left-handed serve down the middle in the second court will curve in toward you, so step in and learn to handle it.

A word of caution: The left-handed serve coming into your right hip can be tough to handle. Stay far enough away so that it doesn't crowd you on the forehand. Above all, watch the ball closely!

The Two-Handed Backhand Hitter

You can use several strategies to defend against a two-handed backhand hitter. Because your opponent does not have as much reach as a one-handed hitter does, you might try to run your opponent wide. You can also hit low angled shots to the backhand so that your opponent will have to let go with one hand to attempt the return. Finally, balls that bounce high are especially difficult for a two-handed hitter to return, so try to hit some of those. Most two-handed backhands are solid and consistent because the preparation is normally straight back and compact. As a result, the two-hander is usually a consistent shot maker with good pace.

Play into the two-handed backhand some of the time, but you might be more successful hitting to their forehand.

Final Thoughts

As the match progresses, pay attention to your opponent's ground strokes. Notice which ones are most effective and adjust your game to take those opportunities away. Also, try different strokes to discover what will work best to defeat your rival. Mix up your shots and aim at the weak spots across the net.

Improving Your Doubles Play

*Communicate, encourage, and congratulate your
partner, and you'll probably win more often
and enjoy your doubles more.*

More people over 50 play doubles rather than singles. In doubles, you have less court to cover, and you have a pal as a partner—a person you can lean on and rely on when you're struggling with your game. Winning doubles takes the right partner, good communication, and well-thought-out strategies. In this chapter we'll look at these key aspects of the doubles game.

Both players are in good ready positions.

Picking a Good Playing Partner

When you pick a doubles partner, look for someone who plays hard but who is encouraging and fun to play with. With the right partner, you can talk about different strategies before you go out to play and during a match. You can readily agree on who should serve first on your team, who will play the forehand or right court, and who will play the backhand or left court.

Suppose you miss a shot and say, "Sorry, partner." The partner you don't want says, "Don't say you're sorry, because then I have to say it's OK." None of us ever misses a shot on purpose, so why should your partner get mad at you?

One of the main reasons you're playing tennis past 50 is to have fun, so be sure to pick a partner you enjoy playing with, one with whom you are compatible. You both play hard, trying to win, but you encourage one another as you play.

If you're playing with a fun partner, you never have to play scared. You don't have to worry about missing a shot, because your partner will always be supportive and encouraging. It's a lot more positive to hear your partner say, "That's OK—we'll get it next time," rather than, "Are you ever going to make a return of serve?"

Communication

The best pro doubles teams talk to one another all the time. Sometimes it's about strategy, but often the partners are encouraging one another. That's when good teams play their best tennis. Communicate, encourage, and congratulate your partner, and you'll probably win more often and enjoy your doubles more.

Let's look at some situations that require communication in the doubles game, including moments that demand cooperation, playing in the wind and the sun, and deciding your roles if one of you is a lefty and the other is a righty.

Cooperation

You will likely encounter situations where you'll have to put your heads together to try to get your game back on track. Returning serves and responding to returns of serves are two such situations.

If you're having difficulty returning serve, you might agree that your partner stay back on your opponent's first serve. That way it's not as critical that your return be very low. If your opponent's second serve isn't causing you trouble, have your partner move back up to the net. If you're having trouble returning the second serve, have your partner stay back on that one as well.

With your partner staying back, you might try to hit a lob on your return of serve. Sometimes, after getting a few returns in play, even as lobs, you will regain your confidence and will start making better service returns.

Suppose you serve and follow it to the net, but your opponent returns with an offensive lob over your partner's head. In that case, suggest that your partner stand back a step or so. This will make it more difficult for your opponents to get the lob over your partner's head, and your opponents may have to try some other strategy.

Whenever possible, take your opponents' favorite shots and strategies away from them. This forces them to try something else, which likely won't be their favorite high-percentage shots. This alone will give you a better chance to win.

Playing in the Wind

Suppose you and your pal are playing in windy conditions. You mutually agree that your partner should serve with the wind, and you'll serve against the wind. After a set, you recognize you're having trouble holding your serve because of the wind. Talk to your friendly partner, and suggest you try the opposite in the second set. You serve with the wind, and your partner will try to serve effectively against the wind. It may work, and it may not, but it's worth a try. Friendly partners will readily agree to such suggestions.

Playing in the Sun

When playing on a sunny day, decide together which player will serve with the sun in the eyes and which will serve from the shady end. Try it for a set one way, and if the sun is really giving one server problems, discuss it, and agree to switch for the second set.

If you are right-handed and your partner is left-handed, neither of you will have to serve looking into the sun. This can be a big advantage.

Lefties and Righties

If one of you is a right-hander and the other a left-hander, you will have to discuss which court each player will return from. If the lefty plays the deuce court, you'll have both forehand volleys and both overhand smashes covering the middle. This can be helpful, because one of the best doubles plays is to go down the middle. When your opponents come down the middle, you both will have your solid forehand volley to play the shot.

But, what if the left-hander returns better from the ad court? Then that's where the lefty should play. In doubles, no matter which hand you and your partner favor, you both should try to play from the court where you can best return. You and your pal can discuss it and agree with ease. If neither of you is returning well, you can switch courts at the end of any set.

Days of Play

Here's something else you may have to work out: You both may still have to work for a living. As a result, you may only be able to play only on the weekends and once during the week. See if you and your pal can arrange to play on Wednesday of each week. That way you will never go more than two days without

VERNE HUGHES

Citizenship: United States of America

Best known for: Winning National doubles titles in every 50s to 80s division

© Verne Hughes

Verne Hughes had early success in tennis, lettering in high school, playing number one on the Long Beach Junior College team, then winning tournaments in California. Later he played at the University of Southern California on a tennis scholarship. Although lack of funds kept Hughes from traveling and playing extensively in the open division, he and Mort Ballagh were ranked 7th nationally in doubles.

After turning 45, Verne began to play in senior tournaments. He has won National doubles titles in every division from the 50s through the 85s. Hughes is currently ranked No.1 nationally in the 85's singles division and No.1 in the 80's doubles division with Mervin Miller. In 2000 he won the National 85's singles division on both hardcourt and indoor.

Hughes' other accomplishments include four Grand Slams in doubles and five International Tennis Federation World Cup championships in doubles.

Hughes stresses the importance of choosing good doubles partners. He has played with Carl Busch, Jack Tidball, Gene Mako, Jack Kramer, Mort Ballagh, and Adrian Quist. He has won national tournaments playing with Len Prosser, Elbert Lewis, Robin Hippensteil, John Shelton, George Young, Dan Walker, Mervin Miller, and Gardnar Mulloy.

On being an older player, Verne Hughes has some advice: "Once you are past fifty, you need to do other exercise besides tennis. Set specific times and adhere to your schedule." He emphasizes the importance of stretching.

—Tony Trabert

hitting a tennis ball. Friends are usually pretty good at working things like this out.

Doubles Strategies

Now that you've selected a good partner and chosen a cooperative approach, let's discuss various doubles strategies that might make your game successful and enjoyable.

First Serves

Get as many first serves in as possible. To do this, you might need to reduce your speed on your first serve. If you reduce your speed by adding a little spin, you'll get a higher percentage of first serves into play. Your opponent will be standing farther back on your first delivery than he or she would be on your second delivery. Your spin serve will be moving a little more slowly and your opponent's return will travel a greater distance, allowing you more time to advance to the net. Of course, it helps if you can mix up the locations of your serves to keep your opponent guessing. And once in a while use your hardest serve first to remind your opponent that you have such a weapon.

You may wonder, *Why shouldn't I hit all my first serves hard?* Because you'll get fewer first serves in, and your opponent will have a better chance of making a damaging return from inside his or her baseline on a shorter second serve that bounces higher.

Returning the Serve

Do your level best to return your opponent's first serve. You don't necessarily have to hit the return hard. The very best return is the one you get back low. A low return forces your opponent to volley up—a more defensive volley. If you can make your opponent hit up to you, you will be able to hit down at him or her. This is particularly true if your partner can poach and intercept your opponent's defensive volley at the net.

In doubles, avoid returning a serve down the alley or sending a passing shot down the alley. You might want to go there once in a while, to make your opponents more hesitant to poach, but you should not make it a regular part of your game. If you hit down the alley and your opponent is there to make a volley, you have opened up your court. An angled volley through the middle will be a winner. A volley angled at your partner who is at the net will be difficult for your partner to handle. Some players return down the alley and then run toward the center to try to catch up with the anticipated volley through the middle. When your opponents see you move, they will volley back down the alley for a winner. Go down the alley once in a while to keep your opponent honest, but don't do it very often.

Attack the Weaker Player

Throughout this book, we stress that you should have fun when you play tennis, and that, in the process, you will also get some useful exercise. But while you are playing, try to win. In your effort to win in doubles, hit as many balls as you can at your weaker opponent. The logic is obvious.

If you are playing mixed doubles and the woman is the weaker player (definitely not always the case), you should attack her with as many shots as you can, because she is more apt to make an error or give you an easy ball to put away.

Your opponents might not like that you are hitting all the shots you can at the weaker player. Tough luck! Nothing in the rules says you have to hit as many to the better player as you do to the weaker one.

Hit Down the Middle

Hit the majority of your shots down the middle of your opponents' court. Because the net is the lowest in the middle, you have a better chance to keep your shots low and get them over the net. (Remember, the net is 36 inches high in the middle and 42 inches high at the sidelines.) When you hit the ball down the middle, your opponents may become confused as to who should take the volley. They might even clash rackets, causing an error. Sometimes they stand there and watch the ball go by, each thinking the other was going to make the play.

Hitting your shots down the middle will also cut down the angles for your opponents. You won't open up your side of the court; this will ensure that either you or your partner will have a good chance on your opponents' next shot.

Use the Lob

Use the lob effectively and not sparingly. The offensive lob over the net player's head on your return of serve can work well. The offensive lob can surprise your opponents if they have a tendency to crowd the net. If you are successful in getting the

Good example of teamwork. Fred Stable is wide out of court while his partner, Ilie Nastase, moves to the center to make the backhand volley.

lob over your opponents' heads, you and your partner should dash to the net. If either opponent attempts a ground stroke past you, you will be in a good position to deal with it. If either lobs, you will be in even better shape and in a good spot to employ your strong overhead. Seldom will your opponent, attempting to make a shot running away from the net, be able to hit a winning shot.

The defensive lob comes in handy when you're pulled out of position. If you hit your lob high, your partner at the net will have time to race back behind the baseline to defend against your opponents' smash. If you can get your defensive lob fairly deep, you will keep your team in the point.

Playing the Net

In doubles you'll usually find one opponent at the net and the other at the baseline. You and your partner will also often be in the same positions—one up, the other back. Usually, the rally will be crosscourt for a few shots and then one of the baseliners will decide to hit at the net person. Unless you're well inside your court so that you can overpower your opposing net person with a hard ground stroke, this is a bad play. Don't hit at the net player from the baseline because your opponent's volley will be angled down at your partner's feet or through the middle. Don't open up your court.

In the same situation, rarely try to lob the ball over the net person's head if one is up and one is back. Unless it's a perfect lob, the smash will come down hard at your partner's feet. Point lost! The best thing to do is continue rallying crosscourt, trying to hit your shots as deep as you can. When you get a short reply, approach with a deep ball crosscourt, and get into your normal volleying position, slightly closer to the service line than to the net.

You and your partner should try to advance to the net together. You will be two "kings of the hill" once you're both positioned at the net. This naturally puts a lot of pressure on your opponents—a lot of bad things can happen to them. They have to worry about the net when trying to get their shots back low at your feet. They have to worry about hitting wide or long over your baseline. They have to worry about both of you making good volleys or smashes if they aren't able to produce extra good shots.

Although you won't win all the points simply because you both arrive at the net at the same time, the odds are in your favor, whereas your opponents have all the things to worry about. In essence, you dictate policy from a net position.

If you decide to poach to intercept the return of serve, make certain you move diagonally toward the net so that you can hit your volley with the ball higher over the net from a position close to the net. When you have that high volley, make sure you hit down at the feet of your opponent at the net. This will win the point for you every time. If the return is lower than the top of the net, you should volley to your opponent at the baseline. Don't volley a low ball up to the net player. If you do, be prepared to eat it!

Hitting the ball down at the feet of your opponent at the net is definitely safer than hitting an angled volley because the shot doesn't have to be as precise. Drive the volley down through the area where your opposing net player is standing for a winner.

In short, when you have a volley above the net, volley down at the feet of the closest opponent. If you have a low volley, volley back to the opponent farthest away.

Suppose you and your partner are at the net, and one of your opponents hits an offensive lob over your head. Your partner yells, "I've got it!" and runs behind you to track down the lob. You need to immediately switch over to your partner's side so that your entire court is covered. Your partner is smart and understands doubles, so up goes a high defensive lob. That's your signal to retreat behind the baseline to prepare to defend against the smash that is certain to come.

Whose Shot Is It?

Good doubles teams communicate well. "Mine," "Yours," "Take it," and "I've got it" should be used frequently. Communicating will help partners know who will take which shots, removing the guesswork from your play.

When you're both at the net, and your opponent hits a shot down the middle, who should take it? The rule of thumb is that the partner crosscourt from where the ball is coming should hit the volley. If your opponent playing the ad court hits the ball toward the middle of your court, the partner in your ad court should make the play. The ball is going toward that player, and away from the partner in the deuce court. If your opponent playing the deuce court hits the ball toward the middle of your court, your partner playing the deuce court should take the volley. Discuss this with your partner so that you are not confused on balls down the middle.

What if both of you are at the net and one of your opponents lobs down the middle? Assuming both you and your partner are right-handed, the player in the ad court should yell, "Mine!" and make the smash. If the player in the deuce court tried to make a play on that lob, it would have to be done with the backhand overhead, which wouldn't be nearly as powerful as the overhead smash of the right-hander in the ad court.

Court Position

Plan your court position strategy ahead of time. Discuss in advance what will happen if one player is at the net, the other is on the baseline, and the net person moves toward the center service line to make a volley. Try to agree that if the net player doesn't cross the center service line, the net player will go back to the original side, and the other player will stay on the same side where he or she started.

However, if the net person crosses the center service line to make a volley, he or she should continue across to get in position on the other side of the court. When the other player sees the net player cross the center service line, he or she should immediately move to the other side to cover that half of the court. Having this understanding ahead of time will take the guesswork out of your positioning. If you cross the center service line, don't double back, because you will double-cross your partner.

So often in mixed doubles, the husband says to his wife, "Get close to the net so that you can touch it with your racket, and get over into the alley. I'll take care of the rest." Wrong! A great player may be able to cover that much court, but the husband is probably not that good. In doubles, you basically want to cover your half of the court and let your partner cover the other half. Remember when you are at the net, you should be a little closer to the service line than to the net. You should stand in the middle of your half of the court so you have equal distance to cover to the left or to the right. Then have fun doing the best you can!

Keep 'Em Guessing

When you are at the net and your partner is serving, there are three actions you can take, although most teams only use two. First, you can stand still when your partner serves. Second, you can poach in an effort to intercept the return of serve. You have probably done both of these things. In addition, consider a third option: Use a fake.

As your opponents are about to return the serve, fake as if you are going to poach but remain in your original position. This can be very disconcerting to your opponents. If you never use the fake, as soon as your opponents see you move, they will know you are crossing the court and they'll hit a winning return down your alley.

If you use the fake occasionally, you may convince your opponents that you are crossing and entice them to hit down your alley. When the return comes to the alley, a volley angled through the middle of your opponents' court is likely to be successful. When you fake, don't be surprised if your opponent hits down your alley. Be prepared because that is why you faked in the first place. Stand still, poach, and fake. Keep 'em guessing.

Final Thoughts

There's a lot of cat and mouse in good doubles play. When do you poach? When do you fake? When do you use the offensive lob? When do you try to surprise the opponent with an occasional shot down the alley?

Double play requires a lot of thought, a lot of planning and more planning. Try it all. What you try won't work all the time, but it will make your doubles matches more challenging, more interesting, and most of all, more fun!

Bibliography

Allen, L.H.O, & S. Margen: Protein-induced hypercalciuria: A longer term study. *American Journal of Clinical Nutrition.* 32: 741-749 (1979).

American College of Sports Medicine: Position stand. The recommended quantity and quality of exercise for the development and maintenance of cardiorespiratory and muscular fitness, and flexibility in healthy adults. *Medicine and Science in Sports and Exercise.* 30(6): 975-991 (1998).

American Dietetic Association: Nutrition for physical fitness and athletic performance for adults: Technical support paper. *Journal of the American Dietetic Association.* 87(7): 934-939 (1987).

Belko, A.Z.: Vitamins and exercise—an update. *Medicine and Science in Sports and Exercise* (Suppl.). 19(5): S191-S196 (1987).

Blom, P.C.S., A.T. Hostmark, O. Vaage, K.R. Kardel, & S. Maehlum: Effects of different post-exercise sugar diets on the rate of muscle glycogen synthesis. *Medicine and Science in Sports and Exercise.* 19(5): 491-496 (1987).

Boles, T. How to relieve a muscle cramp. *Your Patient and Fitness.* May/June: 144 (1992).

Brown, M.B. (March 21, 1997). Flexibility assessment for seniors. Paper presented at the National Convention of the American Alliance for Health, Physical Education, Recreation and Dance, St. Louis.

Burke, L.M., & R.S.D. Read: Sport nutrition: Approaching the nineties. *Sports Medicine.* 8(2): 80-100 (1989).

Charkravarty, K., & M. Webley: Shoulder joint movement and its relationship to disability in the elderly. *The Journal of Rheumatology.* 20: 1359-1361 (1993).

Chilibeck, P.D., G.J. Bell, R.P. Farrar, & T.P. Martin: Higher mitochondrial fatty acid oxidation following intermittent versus continuous endurance exercise. *Canadian Journal of Physiology and Pharmacology.* 76(9): 891-894 (1998).

Clarkson, P.M.: Minerals: Exercise performance and supplementation in athletes. *Journal of Sports Sciences.* 9: 91-116 (1991).

Fleck, S.J., & W.J. Kraemer: *Designing resistance training programs.* 2d ed. Champaign, IL: Human Kinetics (1997).

Fox, E.L. Interval training. *Bulletin of Hospital Joint Disease.* 40:64-71 (1997).

Haymes, E.M.: Protein, vitamins, and iron. In M.H. Williams (ed.), *Ergogenic aids in sports.* Champaign, IL: Human Kinetics, 27-55 (1993).

Hedrick, A.: Dynamic flexibility training. *NSCA Journal.* 22(5): 33-38 (2000).

Karp, J.R.: Interval training for the fitness professional. *NSCA Journal.* 22(4): 64-69 (2000).

Kraemer, W.J., M.R. Deschenes, & S.J. Fleck: Physiological adaptations to resistance exercise: Implications for athletic conditioning. *Sports Medicine.* 6: 246-256 (1996).

Kroculick, S.T.: Carb loading: How to look full and ripped on contest day. *Ironman.* December: 152-153 (1988).

Laiemohn, W., L.B. Snodgrass, & G.L. Sharpe: Unresolved controversies in back management—A review. *The Journal of Orthopaedic and Sports Physical Therapy.* 9: 239-244 (1988).

Lemon, P.W.R., & F.J. Nagle: Effects of exercise on protein and amino acid metabolism. *Medicine and Science in Sports and Exercise.* 13(3): 141-149 (1981).

Lemon, P.W.R.: Nutrition for muscular development of young athletes. In C. V. Gisolfi & D. R. Lamb (eds.), *Perspectives in exercise science and sports medicine.* Indianapolis: Benchmark, 369-400 (1989).

Levin, S.: Investigating the cause of muscle cramps. *The Physician and Sports Medicine.* 19(7): 111-113 (July 1993).

Magee, D.J.: *Orthopedic physical assessment.* Philadelphia: W. B. Saunders, (1992).

Maughn, R.J.: Fluid and electrolyte loss and replacement in exercise. *Journal of Sports Sciences.* 9: 117-142 (1991).

Murray, R.: The effects of consuming carbohydrate-electrolyte beverages on gastric emptying and fluid absorption during and following exercise. *Sports Medicine.* 4: 322-351 (1987).

Nose, H.M., G.W. Mack, X. Shi, & E.R. Nadel: Involvement of sodium retention hormones during re-hydration in humans. *Journal of Applied Physiology.* 65(1): 332-336 (1988).

Pearson, D.: The National Strength and Conditioning Association's basic guidelines for the resistance training of athletes. *NSCA Journal.* 22(4): 14-27 (2000).

Plowman, S.H., & D.L. Smith: *Exercise physiology for health, fitness, and performance.* Boston: Allyn and Bacon, 328-350 (1997).

Reimers, K.: Evaluating a healthy, high performance diet. *Strength and Conditioning.* 16(6): 28-30 (1994).

Rikli, R.E. & C.J. Jones: Development and validation of a functional fitness test for community-residing older adults. *The Journal of Aging and Physical Activity.* 7: 129-161 (1999).

Rikli, R.E. & C.J. Jones: Functional fitness normative scores for community-residing older adults, ages 60-94. *The Journal of Aging and Physical Activity.* 7: 162-181 (1999).

Stanford, B.: Muscle cramps, untying the knots. *The Physician and Sports Medicine.* 19(7): 115-116 (1993).

Steen, S.N.: Nutrition for young athletes: Special considerations. *Sports Medicine.* 17(3): 152-162 (1994).

Stone, M.H., & H.S. O'Bryant: *Weight training: A scientific approach.* Minneapolis: Burgess (1987).

Vander Beek, E.J.: Vitamin supplementation and physical exercise performance. *Journal of Sports Science.* 9: 77-89 (1991).

Vander Beek, E.J.: Vitamins and endurance training: Food for running or faddish claims? *Sports Medicine.* 2: 175-197 (1985).

Wathen, D., & F. Roll: Training methods and modes. In T.R. Baechle (ed.), *Essentials of strength training and conditioning.* Champaign, IL: Human Kinetics, 403-415 (1994).

Witchey, R.L. (1999). The benefits of tennis on functional fitness in older adults. Presented at the USTA Teachers Conference, New York City, (1999) and the Society of Tennis Medicine & Science Annual Meeting, Indian Wells, CA. (1999).

Zatsiorsky, V. *Science and practice of strength training.* Champaign, IL: Human Kinetics (1995).

Zawadzki, K.M., B.B. Yaspelkis III, & J.L. Ivy: Carbohydrate-protein complex increases the rate of muscle glycogen storage after exercise. *Journal of Applied Physiology.* 72(5): 1854-1859 (1992).

Index

Note: The italicized *f* following page numbers refers to figures.

A

assessments, fitness level
 aerobic endurance 35, 36*f*
 agility and balance 37
 flexibility, lower-body 38*f*, 39
 lower-body strength and
  endurance 32*f*, 33
 strength and endurance,
  upper-body 34*f*, 35
 upper-body flexibility 39, 40*f*,
  41

B

backhand
 grip 63-64
 one-handed 64-65
 two-handed 65, 68
Ballagh, Mort 135
Bundy, May Sutton 67
Busch, Carl 135

C

cardiovascular endurance
 defined 73
 interval training 82-83, 86
Cheney, Dorothy (Dodo) Bundy
  66-67
circuit-training
 on-court program 79-80
 guidelines 78-79
 program 77-78
 varying and monitoring 81-82
conditioning
 about 72
 benefits 73
 cardiovascular endurance
  training 82-83, 86

definitions 72-73
 flexibility training 86-96
 muscular endurance training
  77-82
 playing after injury 74
 recovering 96-97
 research 73-74
 strength training 74-77
Connors, Jimmy (James Scott)
  112-113
cramps. *See* muscle cramps

D

dinker
 approach shot 118
 drop shot 118
 offensive lob 119
 second serve 122
 short shots 119, 122
doubles, communication
 about 131-132
 cooperation 132
 days of play 133, 136
 lefties and righties 133
 playing in sun 133
 playing in wind 132-133
doubles, picking partner 131
doubles strategies
 actions at net 142
 court position 141-142
 first serves 136
 hitting down middle 137-138
 playing net 139-140
 returning serve 136-137
 using lob 138, 139
 weaker player, attacking 137
 who takes shot 140-141

drop shot
  backspin 55
  improving 56
  positioning yourself 55-56
  returning 56-57

E

eating for competition
  caloric intake 101
  diet 100
  essential nutrients 102-110
  guidelines 110-111, 114
  muscle cramps 114-115
  nutrition goals 100-101
eating while training
  about 110-111
  after match 114
  before and during match 111
endurance
  cardiovascular 73
  muscular 72-73
equipment
  racket 16-18
  racket grip 22-24
  shoes 25
  strain and pain 24
  strings 18-19, 22
  tennis balls 25-26

F

fitness and game, assessing
  analysis chart 31
  fitness and playing tennis 41
  fitness level 30, 32-41
  game play 30
  strokes 28-30
flexibility training
  about 86-87
  dynamic stretching 92-95
  flexibility, defined 73
  static or slow stretching 87-92
  stretching 96
  warm-up 87
footwork
  moving to ball 68-69
  ready position 68
  split step 69, 69f, 70

G

Goolagong (Cawley), Evonne 20-21
grips
  continental 46, 48, 49
  Eastern forehand grip 46, 48
  semi-Western 46, 48-49
  two-handed backhand 46, 47, 49
  Western 3, 46, 47, 49

H

Hippensteil, Robin 135
hitter, hard
  serving against 123, 126
  tips for playing 122-123
Hughes, Verne 134-135

I

interval training
  about 82
  benefits 82-83
  guidelines 83, 86
  on-court 86

J

Journal of the American Dietetic Association (water guidelines) 108-109

K

King, Billie Jean 12-13
Kramer, Jack 135

L

Laver, Rodney George 124-125
Lewis, Elbert 135
lob
  defensive 58
  mixing it up 59-60
  offensive 57-58
  shots you don't like 58-59
lob, returning
  defensive 61-62
  looking into sun 62
  offensive 60-61
  recovering after smash 62-63

M

Mako, Gene 135
mental toughness
   obstacles overcoming 11
   strategies 11, 14
Miller, Mervin 135
minerals
   macrominerals 106-108
   microminerals 106
Mulloy, Gardner 84-85, 135
muscle cramps, causes 114-115
muscular endurance training.
   See circuit-training

N

Nastase, Ilie 119, 138
nutrients, essential
   carbohydrates 102-103
   fat 104
   minerals 106-108
   protein 103-104
   vitamins 104-106
   water 108-110

O

opponents, strategies
   dinker 118-119, 122
   hard hitter 122-123, 126
   lefty 126
   two-handed backhand hitter
     126-127
opponents, studying 2-3

P

playing smarter
   clay courts 10-11
   explained 2
   mental toughness 11, 12
   net, six-inch difference 10
   racket spin 4
   returns, choosing 5-7
   serve, receiving 4-5
   spin strategies 8-9
   strengths and weaknesses 3-4
   volley position 8
   warm-up 2-3
Prosser, Len 135

Q

Quist, Adrian 135

R

racket
   head size 17-18
   length 17
   swing speed 16-17
   weight 18
racket grip
   grip size 22-23
   small 24
returns, choosing
   backhand, hitting 7
   hitting deep 5-6
   rally, selecting shots 6-7
   shots you don't like 7
Riggs, Bobby 13

S

serve
   swing 51
   the toss 50-51
Shelton, John 135
Smith, Stan 120-121
spin strategies
   slicing serve 9
   standing wider 9-10
   wide delivery 9
Stable, Fred 138
strength, muscular 72
strength training
   benefits 74-75
   guidelines 75-77
   risks 75
stretching, dynamic
   explained 92-93
   lunge walk 93, 93*f*
   torso twists 95, 95*f*
   walking high knee/opposite
     arm swing 95, 95*f*
   walking knee tuck 94, 94*f*
   walking side lunge 94, 94*f*
stretching, static or slow
   calf stretch 92*f*
   chest stretch 89, 89*f*
   explained 88

stretching, static or slow
(continued)
   forearm stretch 90, 90*f*
   lower-back and leg stretch
     91, 91*f*
   shoulder stretch 88, 88*f*, 89
   upper back stretch 89, 89*f*
   upper quads stretch 92, 92*f*
strings
   gauge 22
   tension 19, 22
   types 19
strokes, analyzing
   arms and hands 29
   feet and legs 28-29
   head 29
   hips and shoulders 29
strokes, hitting
   backhand 63-65, 68
   basic grips 46-49
   drop shot 55-56
   footwork 68-70
   ground strokes 52
   lob 57-63
   returning drop shot 56-57
   serve 50-51
   volley 52-55

T
tennis, later life *vii*
Tidball, Jack 135

V
vitamins
   explained 104-105
   intake concerns 105-106
   training 105
volley position
   other volleys 8
   taking lob away 8
volleys
   angled volleys 54-55
   approach shot 52-53
   improving 53-54
   volleying position 53
   wrist 54

W
Wade, Sarah Virginia 42-43
Walker, Dan 135
water
   gastric emptying 110
   intake guidelines 108-109
   intestinal absorption 110
   vs. sports drinks 109, 110

Y
Young, George 135

About the Authors

Now a 50-plus player himself, **Tony Trabert** has been playing tennis since he was six years old. He was the top-ranked player in the world in 1953 and 1955 and was just named president of the International Tennis Hall of Fame. Trabert won three of four Grand Slams, missing only the Australian Championships, and 10 majors in singles and doubles including Wimbledon and the U.S. and French Championships (now referred to as Opens). Trabert played for the Davis Cup team five times with one win and later served as Davis Cup captain for five years with the team winning twice.

He currently works as a television commentator for CBS Sports and Nine Network Australia. He has covered the U.S. Open since 1973 and Wimbledon since 1986, as well as the French Open at Roland Garros, and he's written two books on tennis. He knows many other players of renown who've continued playing into their 70s and 80s—some of whom are featured in this book. He and his wife, Vicki, are residents of Ponte Vedra, Florida.

Ronald L. Witchey is a biomechanist with a specialization in aging and tennis. His research on the benefits of tennis playing on functional fitness in older adults has been presented at the United States Tennis Association (USTA) Teachers Conference, the annual meeting of the Society of Tennis Medicine and Science, and the National Strength and Conditioning Association's Sport-Specific Training Conference. He has also given numerous talks on circuit training, sports medicine, and biomechanics.

A lifetime member of USTA and a former member of the USTA Sport Science Committee, Witchey is the former head men's tennis coach at California State University at Fullerton, where he has been a professor in the division of kinesiology and health promotion for the past 37 years. He's currently the fitness director at SeaCliff Golf and Tennis Club, and he continues to teach biomechanics and anatomy at California State University.

Witchey holds a PhD in kinesiology from the University of Southern California. He lives in Placentia, California, with his wife, Ceci.

Don DeNevi, author of more than 30 books, earned his EdD from the University of California at Berkeley. DeNevi plays tennis as often as he can at the Pebble Beach Tennis Club. He resides in Stockton, California.